The *Yoga Sutra of Patanjali*

LIVES OF GREAT RELIGIOUS BOOKS

FORTHCOMING

The *Yoga Sutra of Patanjali*

A BIOGRAPHY

David Gordon White

PRINCETON UNIVERSITY PRESS

Princeton and Oxford

Copyright © 2014 by Princeton University Press
Published by Princeton University Press, 41 William Street,
Princeton, New Jersey 08540
In the United Kingdom: Princeton University Press, 6 Oxford Street,
Woodstock, Oxfordshire OX20 1TR

press.princeton.edu

Cover illustration by Daren Magee
Cover design by Matt Avery / Monograph

The Swami Shankarananda poem that appears in chapter 1 is reprinted by
permission from *Yoga Philosophy of Patanjali*, by Swami Aranya Hariharananda, the State University of New York Press © 1984, State University
of New York. All Rights Reserved.

First paperback printing, 2019
Paperback ISBN 9780691197074
Cloth ISBN 9780691143774
LCCN: 2013042270

British Library Cataloging-in-Publication Data is available

This book has been composed in Garamond Premier Pro

Printed on acid-free paper. ∞

Printed in the United States of America

CONTENTS

Alberuni, also known as Abu al-Rayhan Muhammad ibn Ahmad al-Biruni (973–1048). A renowned Muslim scientist and court scholar, in 1017 Alberuni was taken by force to India where he authored a learned account of Indian science, culture, and religion titled the *Tahqiq-i-Hind* ("India"), as well as an Arabic translation of a now lost commentary on the *Yoga Sutra*, known today as the *Kitab Patanjal* ("Patanjali's Book").

Aranya, Hariharananda (1869–1947). The author of the most highly regarded twentieth-century commentary on the *Yoga Sutra*, the 1911 Bengali-language *Bhasvati* ("Dawning Sun"), Aranya was also the founder of the Kapil Math monastery in modern-day Jharkand state, where at his request he was sealed into a cave in 1926. He remained there until his death in 1947.

Bhoja, also known as Bhojaraja, Bhojadeva, and Raja Bhoja (eleventh century). The king of the west central Indian kingdom of Malava, Bhoja was the author of the *Rajamartandavritti* ("Royal Sun Commentary") on the *Yoga Sutra*. An enlightened despot, he was also a prolific scholar, patron of the arts, military strategist, and hydraulic engineer.

Blavatsky, Madame Helena Petrovna (1831–1891). Russian-born cofounder of the Theosophical Society and prolific spiritualist author, Blavatsky popularized Yoga in the West by fusing principles and terminology from the *Yoga Sutra* and other works on Yoga with the Western spiritualist ideas of animal magnetism, harmonial religion, and the occult.

Colebrooke, Henry Thomas (1765–1837). British Orientalist and cofounder of the Royal Asiatic Society, Colebrooke authored the earliest English-language scholarly study of the *Yoga Sutra* in 1823. His massive collection of Sanskrit manuscripts, donated in 1818, formed the core of the India Office Library's original manuscript holdings.

Eliot, T. S. (1888–1965). Eliot, who read Sanskrit with James Haughton Woods at Harvard in 1911–12, became fascinated with the *Yoga Sutra* and incorporated its teachings into his psychology of reading and writing as well as, perhaps, into the opening verses of his 1922 masterwork, *The Waste Land*.

Hegel, Georg Wilhelm Friedrich (1770–1831). German Idealist philosopher who adapted Colebrooke's study of the *Yoga Sutra* into his world history of philosophy. For Hegel, Patanjali's Yoga system epitomized the Indian mind, which for him was "prephilosophical," mired in a sort of dreamlike consciousness. Behind his cavalier use of Colebrooke, Hegel's critique of the *Yoga Sutra* was especially a means for him to settle scores with the German Romantics, for whom ancient India was the fountainhead of all wisdom and spirituality.

Hemachandra (1089–1172). A royal minister to the Chalukya king Kumarapala, Hemachandra was a prolific author whose *Yogashastra*, the most comprehensive Jain work on Yoga, drew heavily upon the *Yoga Sutra*.

Hiranyagarbha ("Golden Embryo"). Name of the Hindu creator god who was, according to the *Mahabharata* and several Puranas, the mythical founder of the Yoga system. These same scriptures ignore Patanjali entirely.

Krishnamacharya, Tirumalai (1888–1989). The yoga master of the Mysore Palace's Yogashala, at which he trained three of the most illustrious modern-day gurus of postural yoga, Krishnamacharya was the author of two Kannada- and two Sanskrit-language works on yoga that combined references to the *Yoga Sutra* and the direct revelations he received from a tenth-century Shrivaishnava theologian with instruction in the asanas.

Madhava, also known as Sayana Madhava (d. 1387). A royal minster in the south Indian Vijayanagara kingdom, Madhava wrote a comprehensive account of

Patanjali's system in his *Sarvadarshanasamgraha* ("Compendium of All the Systems"). In spite of the fact that he ranked Patanjali's system higher than all but the Vedanta system, Madhava nonetheless introduced into his commentary several principles of Yoga not found in the *Yoga Sutra*.

Mitra, Rajendralal (1823–1891). An accomplished university-trained Bengali scholar, Mitra authored the first truly complete and comprehensive translation of the *Yoga Sutra* (with Bhoja's commentary) in 1883. Mitra's erudite introduction to the volume remains a valuable resource for Patanjali's biography and philosophical system.

Patanjala, Rishi. Mythical Pashupata teacher and author of the *Dharma Patanjala*, a tenth-century work in Old Javanese that paraphrased nearly the entirety of the first three books of the *Yoga Sutra*.

Patanjali (first century BCE or fourth century CE). Name of the author-compiler of the *Yoga Sutra*, as well as of commentaries on Panini's Sanskrit grammar and the ayurvedic *Charaka Samhita*. According to twelfth-century Tamil temple traditions, Patancali was the name of a half-human half-serpentine incarnation of the great serpent Ananta; later south Indian scholars would go on to identify this mythic figure with the Patanjali of *Yoga Sutra* tradition.

Saraswati, Dayananda (1824–1883). Shaiva monk and founder of the Hindu reform movement known as the Arya Samaj, with which the Theosophical Society briefly merged to form the "Theosophical Society of the Arya Samaj" between 1878 and 1882. In 1848, Saraswati embarked on an unsuccessful nine-year search across India to find an authentic practitioner of Yoga.

Shankaracharya, also known as Shankara (eighth century). A renowned Advaita Vedanta philosopher, Shaiva theologian, and author of numerous commentaries on classical Hindu works, Shankaracharya became the object of several late medieval legendary traditions concerning his "conquest" of India through debate, supernatural powers, and institutional organization. While Shankaracharya may have been the author of a *Yoga Sutra* commentary titled the *Patanjalayogashastrabhashyavivarana* ("Exposition of the Commentary on the Yoga Teaching of Patanjali"), a number of scholars consider this to have been the work of another Shankara, who lived in the fourteenth century.

Vachaspati Mishra (ninth century). Prolific commentator and author of the *Tattvavaisharadi* ("Expert Guide to the True Principles"), considered the most learned, balanced, and comprehensive of all *Yoga Sutra* commentaries.

Vijnanabhikshu (sixteenth century). A renowned philosopher of the Qualified Nondualist school, Vijnanabhikshu was the author of two highly influential

Yoga Sutra commentaries, the *Yogavarttika* ("Explanation of Yoga") and the *Yogasarasamgraha* ("Short Statement on the Essence of Yoga"). Vijnanabhikshu's commentaries greatly undermined earlier understandings of the *Yoga Sutra*'s metaphysics, particularly with respect to Patanjali's teachings on Ishvara.

Vivekananda, Swami (1863–1902). An illustrious Hindu reformer who combined the reform agenda of the Brahmo Samaj with the mystic teachings of the Bengali saint Ramakrishna, Vivekananda was the founder of the Vedanta Society in New York in 1895 and the Ramakrishna Mission in India in 1897. His wildly successful 1896 book, *The Raja Yoga*, which contained an English-language commentary on the *Yoga Sutra*, lit the spark for the enduring Western fascination with Yoga.

Vyasa (also known as Veda Vyasa). The mythic "editor" of the Vedas and *Mahabharata*, Vyasa is also considered by many to be the fourth- or seventh-century author of the "Bhasya," the authoritative commentary on the *Yoga Sutra* that all later commentators took as the basis for their subcommentaries. Several scholars maintain that Vyasa was simply a pen name Patanjali himself adopted to elucidate the elliptical aphorisms of his own *Yoga Sutra*.

Woods, James Haughton (1864–1935). Harvard professor of Indian philosophy and author of what is considered to be the most accurate and authoritative translation (published in 1914) of the *Yoga Sutra* together with the commentaries of Bhoja and Vachaspati Mishra.

Yajnavalkya. A mythic Upanishadic sage, Yajnavalkya is cast in the *Mahabharata* as the revealer of an ancient Yoga system founded by Hiranyagarbha. A ninth- to twelfth-century south Indian by the same name was the author of two works that combined the eight-part practice with teachings on Hatha Yoga and Vedanta philosophy, the *Yogayajnavalkya* ("Yajnavalkya's Yoga") and the *Yogi Yajnavalkyasmriti* ("Tradition of Yogi Yajnavalkya").

Yeats, William Butler (1865–1939). A leading poet of the twentieth century and the first Irishman to receive the Nobel Prize for literature, Yeats became a disciple of the Indian guru Shri Purohit Swami in the last years of his life. The two collaborated on English-language translations of several works of Indian spirituality, including the *Yoga Sutra*.

Over the past forty years or so, a theory has been forged in university departments of history and cultural studies that much of what is thought to be ancient in India was actually invented—or at best reinvented or recovered from oblivion—during the time of the British Raj. This of course runs counter to the view most Indians, Indophiles, and renaissance hipsters share that India's ancient traditions are ageless verities unchanged since their emergence from the ancient mists of time. When I began this project, I was of the opinion that "classical yoga"—that is, the Yoga philosophy of the *Yoga Sutra* (also known as the *Yoga Sutras*)—was in fact a tradition extending back through an unbroken line of gurus and disciples, commentators and copyists, to Patanjali himself, the author of the work who lived in the first centuries of the Common Era. However, the data I have sifted through over the past three years have forced me to conclude that this was not the case.

The present volume is part of a series on the great books, the classics of religious literature, works that in some way have resonated with their readers and hearers across time as well as cultural and language boundaries, far beyond the original conditions of their production. Some classics, like the works of Shakespeare for theater, are regarded as having defined not only their period but also their genre, their worldview, their credo. As the sole work of Indian philosophy to have been translated into over forty languages, the *Yoga Sutra* would appear to fulfill the requirements of a classic. But if this is the case, then the *Yoga Sutra* is a very special kind of classic, a sort of "comeback classic." I say this because after a five-hundred-year period of great notoriety, during which it was translated into two foreign languages (Arabic and Old Javanese) and noted by authors from across the Indian philosophical spectrum, Patanjali's work began to fall into oblivion. After it had been virtually forgotten for the better part of seven hundred years, Swami Vivekananda miraculously rehabilitated it in the final decade of the nineteenth century. Since that time, and especially over the past thirty years, Big Yoga—the corporate yoga subculture—has elevated the *Yoga Sutra* to a status it never knew, even during its seventh- to twelfth-century heyday. This reinvention of the *Yoga Sutra* as the foundational scripture of "classical yoga" runs counter to the pre-twentieth-century history of India's yoga traditions, during which other works (the *Bhagavad Gita*, *Yoga Vasistha*, and various texts attributed to figures named Yajnavalkya and Hiranyagarbha) and other forms of yoga (Pashupata Yoga, Tantric Yoga, and Hatha Yoga) dominated the Indian yoga scene. This book is an account of the rise and fall, and latter day rise, of the *Yoga Sutra* as a classic of religious literature and cultural icon.

A word on the formatting of this book is in order. The compact volume you have in front of you is this book's visible portion: thirteen chapters of text, accompanied by short sets of endnotes and suggestions for further reading. The invisible portion of this book, which may be accessed online through http://press .princeton.edu/titles/10193.html, comprises both its complete complement of notes (indicated by symbols in the margins) as well as a full bibliography.

LIVES OF GREAT RELIGIOUS BOOKS

The *Yoga Sutra of Patanjali*

Reading the *Yoga Sutra* in the Twenty-First Century
MODERN CHALLENGES, ANCIENT STRATEGIES

In the United States, where an estimated seventeen million people regularly attend yoga classes, there has been a growing trend to regulate the training of yoga instructors, the people who do the teaching in the thousands of yoga centers and studios spread across the country. Often, teacher training includes mandatory instruction in the *Yoga Sutra* of Patanjali. This is curious to say the least, given the fact that the *Yoga Sutra* is as relevant to yoga as it is taught and practiced today as understanding the workings of a combustion engine is to driving a car.

So the question that must be asked is: why? Why should a string (this is what the word *sutra* means in Sanskrit, the language of the *Yoga Sutra*) of 195 opaque aphorisms compiled in the first centuries of the Common Era be required reading for yoga instructors in the twenty-first century? What could an archaic treatise on the attainment of release through true cognition possibly have to do with modern postural yoga, that is, the postures and the stretching and breathing exercises we call yoga today (about which the *Yoga Sutra* has virtually nothing to say)? The obvious answer, many would say, is in the title of Patanjali's work: what could the *Yoga Sutra* possibly be about, if not yoga?

Yoga has been a transnational word for over two hundred years. The French missionary Gaston-Laurent Coeurdoux equated the "yogam" of India's "yoguis" with "contemplation" in the mid-1700s (although his writings were not published—plagiarized is a more accurate term—until 1816). In his 1785 translation of the *Bhagavad Gita*, the British Orientalist Charles Wilkins did not provide translations for the words "Yog" or "Yogee," for reasons that will become clear later in this book. "Der Joga" has been a German word for well over a century, "il yoga" an Italian word, and so forth. Of course, yoga was originally a Sanskrit word, so one would think it would suffice to open a Sanskrit dictionary to know what yoga is. Since its publication in 1899, Sir Monier Monier-Williams's *Sanskrit-English Dictionary* has been the standard reference work to which both first-year language students and seasoned scholars have been turning for translations of Sanskrit words. And what is it that we find when we turn to the entry "yoga" in this work? Weighing in at approximately 2,500 words, it is one of the longest entries in the entire dictionary, taking up four columns of print. Seventy-two of those words describe the use of the term "yoga" in the *Yoga Sutra*. They read as follows:

†   Application or concentration of the thoughts, abstract contemplation and mental abstraction practiced as a system (as taught by Patanjali and called the Yoga philosophy; it is the second of the two Samkhya systems, its chief aim being to teach the means by which the human spirit may attain complete union with Isvara or the Supreme Spirit; in the practice of self-concentration it is closely connected with Buddhism).[1]

There is at least one error in this definition, which I will return to later, but first, more on the general meaning of yoga. (Throughout this book, I will capitalize the word "Yoga" when I am referring to Yoga as a philosophical system, whereas I will use the lowercase "yoga" for all other uses of the term.) In keeping with the organizing principles of dictionaries of this type, Monier-Williams begins his yoga entry with its earliest and most widely used meanings before moving into later and more restricted usages. In this ordering, his definition of Yoga appears only after a long enumeration of more general meanings, which, reproduced here, read like a list that Jorge Luis Borges might have dreamed up for his "Library of Babel":

> Yoga: the act of yoking, joining, attaching, harnessing, putting to (of horses); a yoke, team, vehicle, conveyance; employment, use, application, performance; equipping or arraying (of an army); fixing (of an arrow on the bow-string); putting on (of armour); a remedy, cure; a means, expedient,

device, way, manner, method; a supernatural means, charm, incantation, magical art; a trick, stratagem, fraud, deceit; undertaking, business, work; acquisition, gain, profit, wealth, property; occasion, opportunity; any junction, union, combination, contact with; mixing of various materials, mixture; partaking of, possessing; connection, relation (in consequence of, on account of, by reason of, according to, through); putting together, arrangement, disposition, regular succession; fitting together, fitness, propriety, suitability (suitably, fitly, duly, in the right manner); exertion, endeavor, zeal, diligence, industry, care, attention (strenuously, assiduously) . . .

Before we leave Sir Monier behind, it should be noted that postures, stretching, and breathing are found *nowhere* here (although they are alluded to in his definition of Hatha Yoga, in a separate entry). With this, let us return to our original question of why it is—when the "*Yoga Sutra* definition" of yoga is not a particularly early or important one, and when the contents of the *Yoga Sutra* are nearly devoid of discussion of postures, stretching, and breathing whereas dozens of other Sanskrit works with "yoga" in their titles are devoted to those very practices—that instruction in the *Yoga Sutra* should be compulsory for modern-day yoga instructors?

We may begin by placing this modern appropriation of Patanjali's work in its historical context. Since the time of its composition, the *Yoga Sutra* has been interpreted by three major groups: the *Yoga Sutra*'s classical Indian commentators; modern critical scholars; and members of the modern-day yoga subculture, including gurus and their followers. A fourth group, conspicuous by its absence, should also be mentioned here. For reasons that we will see, the people traditionally known as "yogis" have had virtually no interest or stake in the *Yoga Sutra* or Yoga philosophy.

A clear fault line divides the groups just mentioned. On the one hand, modern critical scholars, who read the *Yoga Sutra* as a philosophical work, concern themselves nearly exclusively with the classical commentators and their readings of the work's aphorisms. On the other, there are the adherents of the modern yoga subculture, who generally read the *Yoga Sutra* as a guide to their postural practice, but whose understanding of the work is refracted not through the classical commentaries themselves, but rather through Hindu scripture. Here, I am speaking primarily of the great *Mahabharata* epic and the Puranas ("Antiquarian Books"), massive medieval encyclopedias of Hindu thought and practice. As such, these parallel universes of interpretation converge on but a single point; that point being what Patanjali termed the "eight-part practice" (ashtanga-yoga), his step-by-step guide to meditation. However it turns out that the two constituencies nonetheless have diverged over even this small point, in the sense that the classical commentators and critical scholars have judged this to be the least significant portion of the *Yoga Sutra*, while the modern yoga subculture has focused almost exclusively on the eight-part practice. As we will see in the next chapter, most scriptural accounts of the eight-part practice actually subverted Patanjali's teachings, contributing to the virtual extinction of Yoga as a viable philosophical system by the sixteenth century. Then, through a series of improbable synergies, Yoga rose from its ashes in the late nineteenth century to become a cult object for much of the modern yoga subculture.

Unlike the *Mahabharata* and the Puranas, which are anonymous compilations of ancient Hindu sacred lore, the classical commentaries on the *Yoga Sutra* are "signed" works by historical figures. Most scholars believe that the earliest among these, a certain Vyasa, wrote his commentary within decades of the appearance of the *Yoga Sutra*. However, others argue he lived as many as six hundred years after Patanjali: we will revisit the question of Vyasa's dates in the final chapter of this book. The *Yoga Sutra*'s other major commentaries date from between the ninth and sixteenth centuries; however, no commentary was written in defense of the Yoga system after the twelfth century, which may be taken as a tipping point following which the school began to fall into decline (apart from a limited Yoga "revival" in south India, between the sixteenth and eighteenth centuries).

We know from their writing that the great classical commentators were brilliant, immensely cultivated individuals possessed of a thorough grasp of India's traditional treasury of knowledge. Nearly all were philosophers and schoolmen who, writing in the Sanskrit medium, sought to unpack the meaning of Patanjali's aphorisms and defend their readings of its message against the claims of rival thinkers and schools, of which there were many. In addition to educating their pupils in royal courts, brahmanic colleges, hermitages, temples, and monasteries, they would have also taken part in debates on the great questions of the time, carrying forward a practice that dated back to the Vedas (ca. 1500–1000 BCE), the most ancient sources of Hindu revelation. This we know because many of their commentaries retain a debate format, setting forth their adversaries' perspectives in order to subsequently rebut them with their own arguments. Debates could be lively affairs in these contexts, "philosophy slams" whose victors were often rewarded with wealth, position, and glory.

Every great text in India has been the object of one if not several such commentaries. Generally speaking, these are highly technical treatises that analyze the terms and concepts presented in original scriptures such as (for Hindus) the Vedas, Upanishads, *Bhagavad Gita*, and major philosophical works. Here, the mark of a good commentator is his objectivity, his ability to dispassionately make his points about a text in the light not only of the language of the text itself but also of other commentaries that have preceded his own. As such, commentaries are, in addition to being transcriptions of contemporary debates, conversations with their past, where earlier points of discussion are analyzed through careful precedent-based argument. While outright innovation is a rarity in classical commentary, changing philosophical and real-world contexts make for gradual shifts in the perceived meanings of the words and concepts being interpreted, such that over time—and here I am speaking of hundreds, if not thousands of years—the commentarial "big picture" of a given work is gradually altered, sometimes beyond recognition.

One finds a similar situation in Western legal traditions, in what is known as judicial review in the United States. Judicial review assumes that the principal sources of the American legal system—English common law, the Magna Carta, and most importantly, the Constitution—form a living tradition in which judicial precedents are reinterpreted in the light of changing real-world contexts. Fundamental concepts, such as "free speech," "citizenship," and the "right to bear arms," are constantly being tested and retested through judicial review, changing even as they remain the same. As with Patanjali's work, there is no way to go back to the "original intent" of the framers of the Constitution, which is irrelevant in any case, because their world was not the same as ours today. In many respects, critical Yoga scholars are the modern-day homologues of the classical commentators whose works they study.

Over the past forty years in particular, critical scholarship on Yoga has become a growth industry in the American and European academies. In order to be taken seriously in the academy, the critical scholar must work with primary source material, which in the case of the *Yoga Sutra* has meant not only the sutras themselves but also other Sanskrit-language works on Yoga and allied philosophical systems, and, most importantly, the work's classical commentaries. Here, critical Yoga scholarship primarily consists of the painstaking task of parsing the ways that the words and concepts of the *Yoga Sutra* have been interpreted over time, in order to tease out patterns of influence and change. Then follows the process of the critical review of scholarly ideas in academic colloquia and through journal articles, book reviews, and so forth.

A significant number of mainly North American Yoga scholars have also been practitioners of yoga, and many if not most of these were first drawn into the study of the *Yoga Sutra* through their personal practice. Quite often, their readings of the *Yoga Sutra* will fall somewhere in between those of nonpracticing critical scholars and members of the broader yoga subculture. One count on which these scholar-practitioners tend to disagree with their nonpracticing colleagues concerns the importance of Vyasa to a correct understanding of the *Yoga Sutra*. Vyasa was not only the earliest but also by far the most widely quoted of all the classical *Yoga Sutra* commentators. In fact, the great majority of extant *Yoga Sutra* manuscripts contain not only the work's 195 aphorisms but also Vyasa's original interlinear commentary, appropriately called "The Commentary" (*Bhashya*). That our text should require a "skeleton key" is immediately apparent to anyone who would attempt to read its aphorisms: the sutras are so compact and obscure as to be incomprehensible without accompanying explanation. To begin, Patanjali uses several technical Sanskrit terms in ways that are unique to the *Yoga Sutra*. What is more, the language of the sutras is often closer to what has been termed "Buddhist Hybrid Sanskrit"—that is, the Sanskrit of the early Mahayana Buddhist scriptures of the first centuries of the Common Era—than to the classical Sanskrit of nearly every Hindu scripture and commentary. †

Further complicating matters is the fact that there are only four verbs in the entire work! This is where Vyasa's commentary proves to be a precious resource. Complete sentences require verbs, and Vyasa helpfully supplies the missing verbs and a great deal more. This is not an entirely unprecedented situation. In India, the aphoristic style of sutra-type teachings have traditionally been employed as mnemonic devices for reciting and recalling to memory the central tenets of a given philosophical or religious system. However, without the complement of a living guru's teaching, or, failing that, a written commentary, the aphorisms often remain impenetrable. It would appear that they † were enigmatic to the *Yoga Sutra*'s classical commentators as well. As such, nearly every commentary on the work is actually a subcommentary, that is, a treatise that comments on Vyasa's "authorized" interpretation rather than on Patanjali's work itself.

Vyasa's commentary on the *Yoga Sutra* was not, however, entirely neutral or transparent, since he in fact based it on the metaphysics of a different, but related, philosophical system known as Samkhya. This has had an incalculable effect on how people have read the *Yoga Sutra*, because they have actually been reading it through the lens of Vyasa's Samkhya-inflected commentary. So it is that much of what readers take to be

† the *Yoga Sutra*'s basic vocabulary—the words Purusha (literally "the Man" or "Person," but often translated as "Spirit"), Prakriti ("Nature, Matter, Materiality," a feminine word in Sanskrit), buddhi ("intellect"), and ahamkara ("ego")—are virtually absent from Patanjali's work but omnipresent in Vyasa and well over a thousand years of succeeding commentary and scholarship. Edwin Bryant has summarized the situation in the following terms:

† So when we speak of the philosophy of Patanjali, what we really mean (or should mean) is the understanding of Patanjali according to Vyasa: It is Vyasa who determined what Patanjali's abstruse *sutras* meant, and all subsequent commentators elaborated on Vyasa ... It cannot be overstated that

Yoga philosophy is Patanjali's philosophy as understood and articulated by Vyasa.[2]

To give but a single example of the bedeviling problems the *Yoga Sutra* presents for anyone who would try to penetrate its meaning, we may look at the ways in which people have translated its all-important second sutra into English. This, Patanjali's compact definition of Yoga, is composed of four words: yoga-citta-vritti-nirodha. As usual, there are no verbs in this sutra, so we are in the presence of an apposition: yoga = citta + vritti + nirodha. While "citta" has a wide range of meanings in early Sanskrit, the most adequate non-technical translation of the term is "thought." As for "vritti," it means "turning," and is related to the -vert in the English words introvert ("turned inward") and extrovert ("turned outward") as well as invert, subvert, pervert, revert, and so forth. Nirodha is a term meaning "stoppage" or "restraint" in Sanskrit. A simple translation of yoga-citta-vritti-nirodha should then read something like "Yoga is the stoppage of the turnings of thought." But simple is not the first word that comes to mind when looking at the ways people have read this or the other sutras of Patanjali's work. By way of illustration, here is a sampling of twenty-two from among the many, many English translations—by critical scholars, yoga gurus, and everyone in between—of those four words. Note that with four exceptions (translations 8, 10, 15, and 17), the word order of the English translations is yoga-nirodha-vritti-citta:

†	a.	b.	c.	d.
*1. Concentration (yoga)	is the hindering	of the modifications	of the thinking principle.
*2. Yoga	is the suppression	of the functions	of the thinking principle.
*3. Yoga	is the restriction	of the fluctuations	of the mind-stuff.
*4. Yoga	is the shutdown	of the processes	of the mental capacity.
*5. Yoga	is the cessation	of the turnings	of thought.
*6. Yoga	is the stilling	of the modifications	of the mind.
*7. Disciplined meditation	involves the cessation	of the functioning	of ordinary awareness.
*8. We become whole	by stopping	turns.>>	<<how the mind
*9. Yoga	is the cessation	of movements	in the consciousness.
*10. Yoga	is the ability to direct	toward an object and sustain that direction without any distractions.>>	<<the mind exclusively
*11. Yoga	is the cessation	of [the mis-identification with] the modifications	of the mind.
*12. Yoga	is the inhibition	of the modifications	of the mind.
*13. Yoga	is to still	the patternings	of consciousness.
*14. Yoga	is the restriction	of the fluctuations	of consciousness.
*15. Yoga	is preventing	from going around in circles.>>	<<thought

†	a.	b.	c.	d.
	*16. Yoga	is the control	of thought-waves	in the mind.
	*17. Yoga	is the restraining	from taking various forms.>>	<<of the mind-stuff
	*18. Yoga happens	when there is stilling (in the sense of continual and vigilant watchfulness)	of the movement	of thought—without expression or suppression—in the indivisible intelligence in which there is no movement.
	*19. Yoga	is the restraint	of the fluctuations	of the mind.
	*20. Yoga	is the stilling	of the changing states	of the mind.
	*21. Yoga	is the icy silence	of post-disintegration.	
	*22. Yoga	is the control	of the (moral) character	of thought.

Among all of these, it is the fifth, by Barbara Stoler Miller, that comes closest to the "literal" reading of the words in this aphorism. While others may be read more as interpretations than translations, one might be inclined—in an information age in which opinion is so often confused with knowledge—to mix and match different columns in the hope of reaching some sort of consensus, a "Patanjalian definition of Yoga by committee." So, for example, one could, by combining a9 + b21 + c11 + d7, come up with the following: "Yoga is the icy silence of the [misidentification with] the modifications of ordinary awareness." Taking another tack, a12 + b4 + c22 + d15 would yield "Yoga is the shutdown [of] the [moral] character of thought from going around in circles." On the basis of this not entirely scientific exercise, it is safe to conclude that Patanjali's prose opens the way for a cacophony of interpretations sufficient to blow out the eardrums of even the most earnest of seeker every time he or she seeks to find authentic meaning in its sacred chants. Perhaps Swami Shankarananda came closest to the point in a poem he wrote, which appears in the preface to Hariharananda Aranya's excellent *Yoga Philosophy of Patanjali*:

> To catch the mind and keep it still,
> Is no small problem for my porous will;
> As many times as I shut it down,
> Unceasing thoughts on me rebound
> In youth I tried through alcohol,
> To ease my stress and cool my gall;
> In later years I turned to grass,
> The effects were good—but did not last.
> At last with failing hopes I turned,
> To Eastern paths, and my soul yearned
> To scale the mystic heights of bliss.
> Alas, no easy message this.

And now with age and turmoil weary,
All that's left me is this query:
Will heart break or mind implode,
Before my vrittis do nirode.

Given its robust commentarial and critical history and the high esteem in which it and its author are held by scholars, devout Hindus, and the modern-day yoga subculture in both India and the West, one might assume that the *Yoga Sutra* has been, like the Bible for Christians and Jews, a perennial Indian "classic." As will be shown in the chapters that follow, this has not been the case. For several hundred years prior to its "discovery" by a British Orientalist in the early 1800s, the *Yoga Sutra* had been a lost tradition. As a result, scribes had stopped copying *Yoga Sutra* manuscripts (because no one cared to read them) and instruction in Yoga philosophy had been dropped from the traditional Hindu curriculum (because no one cared to recite or memorize the sutras).

In the wake of this long hiatus, the "recovery" that followed the text's rediscovery was a tortured process, generating much sound and fury, often signifying nothing, as its many modern interpreters projected their fantasies, preconceptions, hopes, dreams, and personal agendas onto Patanjali's work in unprecedented ways. As a result, the *Yoga Sutra* has been something of a battered orphan for the better part of the last two centuries, often abused by well-meaning or not-so-well-meaning experts and dilettantes, mystics and pragmatists, reformers and reactionaries who have seized upon it as a source of political, intellectual, or symbolic capital.

Much of the balance of this book will be devoted to tracing the fractured history of these modern appropriations and contestations, which have carried the *Yoga Sutra*'s legacy across the oceans and over the snowy peaks of the Himalayan Shangri-la, zigzagging between Kolkata, London, Berlin, Varanasi, Chicago, New York, Chennai, Mysore, Los Angeles, and many, many, places in between. Most curiously—and this is what sets the *Yoga Sutra* and its philosophical system apart from every other Indian school—is that this is not the first time that Patanjali's work has been carried far beyond the borders of the Indian subcontinent. This had already occurred in the tenth and eleventh centuries, when extensive *Yoga Sutra* commentaries were written in Arabic and Old Javanese. When one adds to these the ever-growing number of *Yoga Sutra* translations, commentaries, and studies currently being published in seemingly every language on the planet (Japanese, Estonian, Turkish, and Polish, to name a few), the picture that emerges is of something entirely new: an Indian scriptural and philosophical tradition that is truly cosmopolitan, embedded in every part of the world, even if only recently rediscovered in the land of its birth. However, before we turn to these non-Indian appropriations of the *Yoga Sutra*, we must first situate Patanjali's work and its original Indian readers in their ancient and medieval contexts.

Patanjali, the *Yoga Sutra*, and Indian Philosophy

At this point, it is necessary to introduce a small number of more or less untranslatable terms, foreign concepts, and names of philosophers and philosophical schools that will reappear throughout the rest of this book: a cast of *Yoga Sutra* characters and concepts. Nonspecialist readers not interested in the arcana of Sanskrit terminology may want to skip over much of this chapter.

The classical Indian commentators viewed the *Yoga Sutra* as a philosophical work, an investigation into the relationship between Spirit and Matter; an account of the workings of the mind and ways of knowing what is true; a study of cause and effect in the workings of the universe; and a guide to salvation. As is the case with every major Indian philosophical school and religious system, these fields of inquiry—ontology (the nature of being), epistemology (what it means to know), psychology (the workings of the mind), cosmology (the shape of the universe), and soteriology (being saved)—

are intertwined. While India has known many, many philosophical schools or systems (darshanas) over the past three millennia, the following six have been singled out, since the sixteenth century, as the "classical" Hindu darshanas: these are Samkhya, Yoga, Nyaya, Vaisheshika, Mimamsa, and Vedanta. The first five of these can be dated back to the last centuries before the Common Era. Three among them—Nyaya ("Logic"), Vaisheshika ("Atomism"), and Mimamsa ("Vedic Exegesis")—are largely irrelevant to the history of the *Yoga Sutra* and its history of interpretation. Samkhya ("Enumeration"), the system with which Yoga philosophy has the most in common, is of great importance. The last, known as Vedanta—because it based itself on the philosophy of the Upanishads, the final collection of teachings within the Vedic canon, which were also known as the "Veda's end" (veda-anta)—emerged several centuries later. While there are three subschools of Vedanta philosophy—Dualist, Nondualist, and Qualified Nondualist—the Nondualist (Advaita) school that the great eighth- to ninth-century Shankaracharya (or Shankara) championed has been by far the most influential in the history of Hindu thought, especially over the past five hundred years. These Hindu systems did not develop in a vacuum however: two other philosophical systems that influenced, and were influenced by, Yoga philosophy were those of early Jainism and Buddhism.

Generally, one wants to begin at the beginning, but as is so often the case with ancient Indian traditions, beginnings can be rather tricky. The *Yoga Sutra* is probably not the first Indian work to be devoted to either yoga or Yoga, although Indian texts are notoriously difficult to date. Generally speaking, Hindu scriptures are broadly divided into Revelation (shruti, literally "that which was heard") and Tradition (smriti, literally "that which was recalled"). The former category covers the Vedas, Brahmanas, Aranyakas, Upanishads, Dharmasutras, and the ritual Sutras, works considered to have been orally revealed to the ancient seers. Generally speaking, these works of Revelation date from between 1500 BCE and 400 CE. The latter category comprises India's two great epics, the *Mahabharata* and *Ramayana*; the law books (called Smritis); and the Puranas and other sectarian works called the Tantras and Agamas.

The earliest extant works on Yoga philosophy fall on the cusp between these two bodies of scripture. Yoga and Samkhya are discussed at some length in the †
Katha Upanishad, a work of Revelation that likely dates from some time between 300 and 100 BCE. Yoga is also the principal focus of the sixth book of another Upanishad, the *Maitri*, which may date from as late as or later than the *Yoga Sutra*. The *Mahabharata* contains extended discussions of yoga and Yoga in its sixth and twelfth books, both of which are also more or less coeval with the *Yoga Sutra*. Some of the epic's earlier books evoke a lost yoga tradition that glorified †
the apotheosis of the dying chariot warrior and his embodied rise up to the world of the gods: in its descrip-

tions of these heroic deaths, the epic used the word "yoga" to denote the heavenly chariot that carried the warrior up through the orb of the sun to the elevated plane of the divine.

The portion of the *Mahabharata*'s sixth book in which Yoga is a prime focus is best known under the name of the *Bhagavad Gita*, which comprises a series of teachings on human responsibility, love of God, and the "three yogas" of action, knowledge, and devotion as revealed by the supreme god Krishna to the epic warrior Arjuna. This work would become the foundation of yoga as practiced by the various Vishnu-worshipping (Vaishnava) traditions, whose many proponents inserted chapters on yoga and Yoga into the Vaishnava Puranas. Several chapters of the *Mahabharata*'s twelfth book are also devoted to Yoga, together with Samkhya. In one of these, a divine figure named Hiranyagarbha ("Golden Embryo") is identified as both a creator god and the primordial revealer of the Yoga system. Certain commentators provide a title for his teachings: *Hiranyagarbhayogashastra* ("Golden Embryo's Treatise on Yoga"); and several sources quote or cite his work, one of them quite extensively. Several Puranas would also identify Hiranyagarbha, rather than Patanjali, as the original revealer of Yoga. However, the bulk of the twelfth book's extensive teachings on Samkhya and Yoga are attributed to Yajnavalkya, an ancient seer with an Upanishadic pedigree. Like Hiranyagarbha, Yajnavalkya is also identified as the author of a number of later works on yoga and Yoga. As we will see shortly, the Puranas would entirely ignore Patanjali in favor of these and other mythic Yoga seers.

The *Mahabharata*'s twelfth book also mentions an early group of Shiva-worshipping (Shaiva) ascetics †
called the Pashupatas, who developed their own form of yoga, called Pashupata Yoga, during the same period. This alternate form of yoga—which persisted alongside Patanjali's Yoga, Tantric Yoga, and Hatha Yoga—is described in detail in the Shaiva Puranas as well as in an Indonesian work titled the *Dharma Patanjala*. We will return to these traditions in chapters 7 and 9.

Like the earlier *Katha Upanishad*, the *Mahabharata* †
presents Yoga and Samkhya together. This is a commonplace of Yoga philosophy: that Yoga is but a variation on Samkhya philosophy, a program of meditation and other techniques erected upon a foundation of Samkhya metaphysics. If only for this reason, most *Yoga Sutra* manuscripts, in their colophons—the "credits" appended to manuscripts in which dates, authors' and commentators' names, and other information are provided—identify the work as an "interpretation of Samkhya" (samkhya-pravachana). From the twelfth century onward, authors would also refer to Patanjali's system as "Samkhya with Ishvara" (seshvara †
samkhya), by way of saying that the Yoga system's sole significant divergence from Samkhya theory concerned "Ishvara." This critical term, which may be translated as "Lord," "Master," or "God," will be discussed in chapter 10.

Now, if Yoga philosophy were originally grounded in Samkhya, then one would expect to find a foundational work on Samkhya predating the *Yoga Sutra*. This is not the case: the earliest comprehensive work on Samkhya, the *Samkhya Karika* of Ishvara Krishna, is thought to date from the same period as the *Yoga Sutra*. Furthermore, as Peter Schreiner argued in a † groundbreaking article, the *Mahabharata*'s presentation of Samkhya appears to presuppose a preexisting Yoga tradition rather than the other way around. Other sources, however, indicate that Samkhya came † first. Most importantly, several traditions concur that a legendary sage named Kapila and his illustrious pupils systematized Samkhya several centuries before the beginning of the Common Era. The names of these sages are also found in the *Mahabharata*.

At bottom, the relationship between Samkhya and Yoga—if indeed the two strands were ever separate from each other—is a chicken and egg question. What we do know is that the centuries prior to the beginning of the Common Era saw the emergence of nearly all of the great Indian philosophical systems, systems of remarkable sophistication and complexity: Jainism, Buddhism, Nyaya, Vaisheshika, Mimamsa, Yoga, and Samkhya. Here, it is essential to understand that in spite of their marked disagreements over issues of ontology, soteriology, and so forth, the proponents of these schools—the authors of their foundational texts and commentaries—all agreed on a great many matters. Not the least of these was that a philosophical system had to be coherent and rigorous at every level. These philosophical systems were unified Theories of Everything, and because everything in the universe is interconnected, everything—knowing, being, being saved, cause and effect, time, space, mind, body, etc. etc.—had to be consistent. In this respect theirs were very much like the current Theory of Everything of modern-day theoretical physics, whose models for the origin of the universe, the fabric of space-time, the relationship between matter and energy, and so forth cannot allow for the slightest flaw or internal contradiction. Otherwise, the perfect mathematical crystal collapses.

Like modern-day theoretical physicists, the ancient commentators were members of an intellectual elite, writing for one another and not for the unwashed masses. They and their philosophical systems, did, however, differ from those of modern theoretical physics on two critical points. The first, and most obvious, is that their motive behind decrypting the workings of the universe was a soteriological one, carried out in the name of freeing humans from the prison of suffering existence. This was an agenda set in the middle of the first millennium BCE, in both the Hindu Upanishads and the foundational scriptures of Buddhism and Jainism, the two highly ascetic "new" religions of ancient India. Because of their soteriological focus, these schools generated a vision of the universe, which, while entirely different from our own, was nonetheless rational, coherent, and verifiable on the basis of their foundational axioms. By the time of the *Yoga Sutra*, all of human knowledge had been organized around this goal, such that each of the leading philosophical systems was able to fully explain and link together all known physical and spiritual phenomena, including reincarnation, memories of past lives, cause and effect, "supernatural" powers, and so forth into a unified whole.

Because, however, their explanations for the unseen forces underlying the visible universe do not correspond to those of modern science, we moderns refer to their systems as metaphysics, as opposed to the mathematically provable laws of physics. This brings us to the second major point of difference between the ancient Indian philosophers and modern-day theoretical physicists. The latter use mathematics, a universal notation system whose signifiers—numbers, equations, algorithms, and so forth—remain constant and transparently equivalent to that which they signify, no matter where or when that language is being written or read. Not so for the Indian philosophers, whose language of expression was Sanskrit, a "perfected" (this is the meaning of the word) language to be sure, but a far less precise mode of expression than the language of mathematics. This is what made commentaries so vitally necessary: in order to demonstrate that the axioms of a given philosophical system were valid, the technical language of those axioms had to be analyzed in hair-splitting detail. For this reason, commentators

† were also attentive to Indian theories of language, of

the power of words to represent reality—or even to (re)create reality, as in the case of the Vedic mantras. Nonetheless, this language-based format has made ancient Indian philosophy terribly fragile, protean, and difficult to grasp for modern-day interpreters. As we saw for the simple definition of Yoga in the last chapter, the translation of terms whose meanings have changed over time is a daunting task. This is also why I compared the work of commentators and scholars to the practice of judicial review in the American legal system. Metaphysical positions that were set forth in words rather than mathematical formulas are more like legal precedents than the postulates of theoretical physics.

With this, let us dwell for a moment on some of the basic principles of ancient Samkhya-Yoga philosophy, which form the context for the bulk of the *Yoga Sutra*'s aphorisms, as well as their commentaries. To begin, this is a Dualist system, comprised of Spirit and Matter. While there are many individual Persons or Spirits, Nature or Matter—which comprises all of the stuff of the universe, including every human body *and every human mind*—is one. Although it is unified, our universe, the stuff of Prakriti, is in constant flux, morphing into a series of twenty-four unstable entities, principles, or substrates, called tattvas. Some of those are more stable than others, and the citta—which, because it is part of matter, is often translated as "mind-stuff"—pulled and stretched in every direction by the senses, is constantly organizing these into "me" (ego, ahamkara), other people, animals, houses, and all the other things in the world. Utterly separate from these is Purusha, the twenty-fifth principle.

Why is all of Nature constantly in flux? It is here that we may see how Samkhya-Yoga, like every other Indian philosophy, functions in the service of salvation, of freeing humans from suffering existence. The goal here is to free the mind from its misconception that the Person or Spirit is trapped in the cycle of death and rebirth. Although all the Persons in the universe are embedded in Matter, they are not subject to its laws: each Person is pure, luminous, transcendent consciousness. Yet it is precisely when it comes into contact or proximity with a Person (also called a "Viewer" or "Spectator" [drastr])—that Nature (also called "What is Seen" [drsya]) is set into motion, evolving and devolving into the various substrates of the phenomenal world, putting on a spectacle for the Spectator to see. Even though Nature, *including the mind-stuff*, is entirely unconscious—with its mutations occurring like the behavior of iron filings around a magnet—the great Shankara's description of Nature as an actress or a dancer is one that many a philosopher has evoked down through the centuries. Even as Nature in its many permutations is unconscious, its "performance" serves a purpose: to stimulate each Person, each "Spectator," to realize that it is not a part of the spectacle it has been watching, that is, to realize its intrinsic "isolation" (kaivalyam) from Her. When this is accomplished, She leaves the stage.

The role of the substrate that Patanjali calls the mind-stuff is absolutely critical here, because it is not only the most immediate interface between the individual Person and the rest of the universe, but also the most volatile. The mind-stuff is the mirror in which the luminous "Spectator" sees itself, but that mirror is a funhouse mirror made of the same stuff as the Terminator in "Terminator Two," altering its shape, form, size, and quality at every moment. Its flux is the result of the mind's ever-changing reactions to sensory stimuli, erroneous conceptions, passions, emotions, memories (both immediate and of past lives), and so forth. These are the "turnings of thought" or "fluctuations of the mind-stuff" (citta-vritti) of the *Yoga Sutra*'s definition of Yoga, which the commentator Vachaspati Mishra interpreted as "mutation into the form of an object." While the form that that mental flux will most often take is that of the transient, death-laden body with which it identifies (by positing an ego), its potential forms, qualities, and extensions are limitless. So it is that when the mind-stuff is drawn away from the body and the senses and toward the pure luminous consciousness of the Person, it seemingly becomes conscious, while in fact it is simply absorbing and reflecting the Person's own mode of being.

In the Samkhya system, the Person's gradual realization of its freedom from the material world, death and rebirth is effected through rational inquiry into each of the substrates through which Nature devolves, all the way down to gross matter, the inert stuff of the body and the universe. These include the five elements, the senses, mind, and ego, culminating in the intellect (buddhi). By fully knowing them, the Samkhya philosopher gradually comes to realize that the Person has no part in them. In Yoga, the method of practice changes to one of concentration, meditation, and introspection, issuing into a direct yogic perception (yogi-pratyaksha) of what truly is, a type of knowledge that is entirely intuitive and nonconceptual, bypassing the "turnings of thought" entirely. At the outset, this involves restraining the activities of the body, followed by breath control, because by stilling the breaths one quiets the senses and stabilizes the mind. Then, through deepening stages of meditation, the practitioner's thinking process or mind-stuff is trained away from the outward stimuli that normally render it so unstable and bound to the lower substrates of Matter, and then toward concentration on the luminous, immobile Person itself. Because the mind-stuff absorbs and reflects the qualities of its increasingly subtle objects, it too becomes increasingly subtle, stable, and expansive. When perfect concentration (samadhi) is achieved, the mind-stuff becomes pure, tranquil, and transparent to pure consciousness, expanding out to the farthest reaches of space to disappear from view. With this, Nature has left the stage, and with nothing left to view, her Spectator, no longer subject to the filtering or distorting effects of the mind-stuff, becomes aware of His isolation from the activities of the material world, and "dwells in His own form." Once its isolation from the flux of suffering existence has been realized, suffering ceases.

Yoga philosophy postulates that the mind-stuff, or more properly speaking, Nature's highest evolute, the intellect, has the power to penetrate anywhere and expand infinitely. This was a subject of sustained discussion in the classical commentarial tradition, and its implications continue to resonate in scholarly circles down to the present day. Here it is essential to note an important distinction between classical Indian and modern Western theories of perception. In the Indian †case, the "thinking principle or intellect assumes the form of the object perceived ... [W]hen it is active and influenced by external objects it assumes the forms of its excitants."[1] The same logically applies to the dimensions of the perceived object, such that when the thinking principle or intellect is observing the outermost and most subtle reaches of the universe, it is simultaneously stretched out to universal dimensions. This principle, already introduced in the *Maha-* †*bharata*, is carried forward in a wide variety of works on Yoga. The implication here is that a yogi's body attains universal dimensions as well: this is one of the su- †pernatural powers of the yogi alluded to in the *Yoga Sutra*'s third chapter.

Once it has been trained through the practice of yogic meditation, the mind-stuff's limitless potential for expansion sets the stage for what are often referred to as the "supernatural powers," the main topic of the *Yoga Sutra*'s third chapter. These include the mind-

† stuff's power to enter into the bodies of other beings,
† the power of flight, invisibility, the ability to read other people's minds, to know one's past and future lives, and knowledge of what is subtle, hidden, and distant. Colophons refer to this as the chapter on *vibhuti*, a word that literally means "the power to extend everywhere." When understood in the context of Samkhya-
† Yoga metaphysics, there is nothing supernatural about these powers. As the mind-stuff absorbs and reflects the Person's luminous power of consciousness, it, like
† consciousness, becomes omnipresent, capable of penetrating or transforming into anything, and cognizant of everything. We will return to the place of these powers in chapter 7.

While all of the major Indian philosophical systems have salvation as their goal, and while most agree that the workings of the mind are both the source and the potential solution to the problem of suffering, they take radically different positions on several essential points. Because we will be returning to it frequently in these pages, one of these—the relationship of the Person (Purusha), or Self (Atman, Brahman) to the material world—must be addressed here. As we have seen, in the Dualist system of Samkhya-Yoga, *both individual Persons (Purushas) and the Matter in which they are embedded are real*, but they are radically separate. Here, the goal of practice is to realize their separateness and thereby free the Person from its imagined entanglements with the material world. In distinction to this, the Nondualist system of Advaita Vedanta maintains that *the universal Self (Brahman) is real but that the material world is unreal.* There is nothing that exists that is not the Self; however, due to "cosmic illusion" (maya), individual selves believe that they are distinct entities, cut off from one another and the universal Self by illusory bodies and the stuff of the world. Here the goal of practice is to realize that all that is not Brahman is an illusion. By truly knowing that all is one and internal to Brahman, the individual self achieves identity with the universal Self, even though in reality it never was truly distinct from it. Finally, according to the Buddha's teachings, *both the individual self and the material world are unreal,* and there is no transcendent Self. There is only suffering, which the "no-self" (anatta) identifies with, due to the wanderings of the mind, which chases after chimerical objects that are its own projections.

This is all heady stuff, ample witness to the fact that the worldview of Patanjali and his classical commentators was very different from our own. For all this, the highly technical philosophical passages of these works are often interspersed with allusions to real-world phenomena that are far more familiar. We have already noted Shankara's comparison of Prakriti to an actress or dancer who puts on a show for Purusha, her passive Spectator. So, too, the metaphor of a magnet and iron filings to evoke the effect of conscious Spirit on unconscious Matter is one that does not give us brain cramps. Some images are quite lovely: the reflection of a flower

in a glass, water sliding through the sluice gate of an ir-
† rigation channel, bees following their queen, a humble
wooden cart carrying a precious, fragrant load of saf-
fron. Notably absent from the *Yoga Sutra* and its com-
† mentaries is the slightest reference to a yogic "lifestyle,"
of living in harmony with nature in a forest existence
or remote monastery, hermitage, or cave.

The place where one would expect to find such references is the most straightforward and user-friendly
portion of the *Yoga Sutra*, the second of its four chapters (padas), which is devoted to practice. Here, two
types of practice are proposed. For the nonspecialist,
there is "practical yoga" (kriya yoga), which has three
parts: asceticism, the study and recitation of sacred
hymns and syllables, and dedication to Ishvara. For the
practitioner questing for liberation from suffering existence, Patanjali introduces the eight-part practice,
which comprises the (1) inner and (2) outer restraints,
(3) posture, (4) breath control, (5) retraction of the
senses, (6) fixation, (7) meditation, and (8) pure con-
† templation. Comprising the final twenty-eight verses
of chapter 2 and the three opening verses of chapter 3,
Patanjali's presentation of the eight-part practice is a
short respite from the highly theoretical focus of the
greater bulk of his work. A compact step-by-step approach to the practice of meditation, it receives limited
attention from the classical commentators. There are
two possible explanations for this general commentarial disregard for practice. The first is that the commen-

tators did not meditate or practice yoga. The second is that although they may have undertaken the eight-part practice in their private lives, their public roles as commentators obliged them to stay on message and to focus on the *Yoga Sutra* as a Theory of Everything.

Standing (or sitting in lotus posture) at the opposite end of the spectrum are the modern-day yoga gurus, who, in their frequent references to the *Yoga Sutra*, rarely refer to any but the thirty-one verses that comprise Patanjali's teaching on the eight-part practice. In so doing they often confuse the part for the whole, presenting the eight-part practice as the "essence" of Yoga, to the exclusion of the work's other 164 verses. The same yoga gurus, as well as some critical Yoga scholars, also tend to assume that Patanjali personally practiced the Yoga described in the *Yoga Sutra*, that he was something more than an intellectual author of a Theory of Everything.

The issue of the historical Patanjali and his relationship to the work attributed to him brings us back to the question of origins. As I have already noted, several yogas were in vogue prior to the composition of the *Yoga Sutra*, and some of these involved meditation. In addition, there were several meditation traditions—those of the Jains and Buddhists in particular—that while they did not call themselves "yoga" certainly anticipated many of the concepts and practices found in Patanjali's work. So it is that some classical commentators and most critical scholars have viewed Patanjali not as an original author, but rather as a compiler who

† wove together at least two—but perhaps as many as six—preexisting Yoga traditions or texts.

King Bhoja, an important eleventh-century commentator, was the first to concern himself—primarily for purposes of self-promotion—with the identity, or
† multiple identities, of Patanjali. "Patanjali" is listed as the name of one of the twenty-six mythical Divine Serpents in a number of Puranas. One of these was the sixth-century *Vishnudharmottara Purana*, a work from Kashmir, where Patanjali has long been particularly revered. According to the *Vishnudharmottara*, "the image of Patanjali's Yoga teaching should have the form of Ananta," Ananta being the name of the divine Lord of Serpents who bears the entire universe upon his thousand outspread cobra hoods. This was noted by Bhoja, who went on to write the following verses of (self-) praise in the introduction to his "Royal Sun" commentary:

† I bow with folded hands to Patanjali, the best of sages, who removed the impurities of the mind through yoga; the impurities of speech through grammar; and the impurities of the body through medicine. To he whose upper body has a human form, who holds a conch and a wheel, who is white and has a thousand heads, to that Patanjali, I offer obeisance. Victory be to the luminous words of the illustrious sovereign [Bhoja] . . . who by creating his grammar, by writing his comment on the Patanjalian [treatise, the *Yoga Sutra*], and by producing

[a work] on medicine ... has—like the Lord of the Protectors of Serpents—removed defilement from our speech and minds and bodies.[2]

This identification of a single figure named Patanjali as the author of foundational works in the three fields of philosophy, grammar, and medicine is not without historical precedent. While it is generally accepted that Patanjali was the author-compiler of a philosophical treatise, the *Yoga Sutra*, there also exist commentaries on two other works that were written by a figure having the same name. One of these is the *Mahabhashya*, the "Great Commentary" on Panini's authoritative Sanskrit grammar, which dates from about the second century BCE. In it, the commentator Patanjali refers to himself as the son of a woman named Gonika, †
a name that resurfaces in a twelfth-century myth. The other, a commentary on the *Charaka Samhita*, a foun- †
dational work on Ayurveda, likely dates to a century or two before Bhoja's time. This timeline makes it highly doubtful that these three Patanjalis could have been one and the same person. In more traditional circles, however, Bhoja's identification has become an oft-repeated article of faith, and his glorification of the three-in-one Patanjali continues to be recited in B.K.S. †
Iyengar Yoga classes around the world.

In the modern-day yoga subculture, the most widely circulated explanation for Patanjali's link to the serpent world is, like so many Indian origin myths, based on an etymology—a linguistic breakdown—of Patanjali's name, which several grammarians derived from the Sanskrit words *patat* ("falling") and *anjali*, the reverentially "joined hands" one sees in the decor of seemingly every Indian restaurant on the planet: "falling into joined hands." In about the twelfth century, a pilgrim's guide to the great temple complex of Cidambaram, the "home of the dancing Shiva," in the south Indian state of Tamil Nadu, provided a narrative to explain this etymology. In the same century, several sculpted images of this half-serpent, half-human Patanjali were carved into the Cidambaram temple's walls; similar images are found in other Shaiva temples of south India. According to this pilgrim's guide, the Lord of Serpents sought rebirth as a human in order to witness Shiva's awesome dance at Cidambaram. When he emerged from her body in a half-human, half-serpent form, his human mother, shocked at the sight of her hybrid offspring, let him fall from her hand. So he was named Patancali, the Tamil equivalent of the Sanskrit Patanjali.

This narrative explanation for the images of Patanjali that a twelfth-century pilgrim would have seen at the Cidambaram temple nonetheless makes no link between the semiserpentine devotee Patanjali and the human author-commentator of the same name, and this in spite of the fact that one of the prayer books used there, the *Patanjali Puja Sutra*, is said by modern-day temple priests to have been composed by Patanjali the grammarian. Also absent from this myth is the identification of the serpent-boy Patanjali's mother as

Gonika. Those connections would not be made until †
the seventeenth century, in the south Indian poet
Ramabhadra Dikshita's *Patanjali Charita* ("Story of
Patanjali"). Then, in the eighteenth century, Maritontadarya, a Shaiva master from the south Indian state of
Karnataka, would identify this mythic Patanjali with
the Yoga philosopher:

> Out of grace to the world and by way of introduc- †
> ing the sciences of yoga and so forth, [the] primal
> [serpent named] Shesha [i.e., Ananta took] the
> form of the seven-year-old son of a brahmin
> woman named Gonika. [By virtue of] "falling into
> her hand," he was named Patanjali.[3]

These late south Indian myths are evidence for a six-
teenth- to eighteenth-century "Yoga revival" in south
India, which, as we will see, may have motivated Iyengar's guru, the great Tirumalai Krishnamacharya, to
study the *Yoga Sutra* in the twentieth century. Apart
from the twelfth-century Patanjali shrine at Cidambaram, there is no historical record of any temple ever
having been dedicated to Patanjali prior to the 2004 †
inauguration of just such a shrine to the author of the
Yoga Sutra by Iyengar in Bellur (Karnataka), the city of
his birth. No doubt inspired by Maritontadarya,
whose work was published in Hubli, a few hundred
miles to the north, in 1936, Iyengar further embel-
lished the story of the serpent-boy Patanjali's birth
into the version known to the same pupils who recite

Bhoja's praise to the three-in-one Patanjali at the start of each of their Ashtanga Yoga classes. Iyengar's retelling takes Ananta-Shesha's witnessing of the dance of Shiva (without the mention of Cidambaram) as its starting point, after which:

† Adisesa [i.e., Ananta] then began to meditate to ascertain who would be his mother on earth. In meditation, he had the vision of a yogini by the name of Gonika who was praying for a worthy son to whom she could impart her knowledge and wisdom. He at once realized that she would be a worthy mother for him, and awaited an auspicious moment to become her son. Gonika, thinking that her earthly life was approaching its end, and that her desire of finding a worthy son would remain unfulfilled; now, as a last resort looked to the Sun God, the living witness of God on earth and prayed to Him to fulfill her desire. She took a handful of water as a final oblation to Him, closed her eyes and meditated on the Sun. As she was about to offer the water, she opened her eyes and looked at her palms. To her surprise, she saw a tiny snake moving in her palms, who soon took on a human form. This tiny male human being prostrated to Gonika and asked her to accept him as her son. This she did and named him Patanjali. *Pata* means falling or fallen and *anjali*. . . means "hands folded in prayer." Gonika's prayer with folded hands thus bears the name Patanjali.[4]

Critical scholars dismiss all of this as mythology, of no value for excavating the historical Patanjali, the man who presumably walked the earth in the early centuries of the Common Era. For many Hindus, however, these myths are highly meaningful, since they lend a cachet of authenticity, if not divine intervention, to the production of our text. If, like Hiranyagarbha in the *Mahabharata*, Patanjali were a god who came down to earth to reveal a divine teaching to the world, then that teaching would count as Revelation (shruti), and as revelation it would have been transmitted orally down the ages, from guru to disciple, through rote recitation. Although there is no hard evidence to prove it, several scholars—as well as Iyengar, Deshikachar, Prabhavananda, Isherwood, and others—believe that this was how the *Yoga Sutra* was traditionally transmitted. It may be that Vyasa also viewed the *Yoga Sutra* as belonging to the canon of revelation; however, for him, Patanjali would merely have been the human transmitter of that revelation and not its divine source.

While I will be referring to over a dozen classical *Yoga Sutra* commentators in this book, five stand out in terms of their antiquity and importance. Four of these have already been mentioned: Vyasa, Shankara, Vachaspati Mishra, and Bhoja. Here, some background on these men and their works, as well as on the fifth great *Yoga Sutra* commentator, Vijnanabhikshu, is in order. We have already begun to look at issues surrounding the relationship between Vyasa's "Commen-

tary" and the *Yoga Sutra*, with the majority scholarly
opinion being that Vyasa was a near contemporary of
† Patanjali. A significant minority opinion, however,
maintains that Vyasa lived several centuries later, and
that his "Hindu-izing" commentary, rather than elucidating Patanjali's text, actually subverted its original
"Buddhist" teachings. I will return to this provocative
hypothesis in the final chapter of this book.

Following Vyasa was another commentator whose
identity has also been a source of disagreement among
critical scholars. This is Shankara, whom some identify
with Shankaracharya, the illustrious ninth-century
Advaita Vedanta theologian, commentator, debater—
and, according to legend, the founder of a confedera-
tion of brahmanic religious orders known as the Dandins or Dasnamis. An intellectual giant, Shankara
wrote commentaries on several essential religious and
philosophical works, including an early Upanishad,
the *Bhagavad Gita*, the *Samkhya Karika*, and the
Brahma Sutra. Many of the traditions surrounding
Shankara are apocryphal, including, for some scholars,
the claim that the Shankara authored a work titled the
Patanjalayogashastrabhashyavivarana ("Exposition of
the Commentary on the Yoga Teaching of Patanjali").
Like Patanjali, Shankara is a relatively common name,
and so this too may have been a less illustrious Shan-
† kara. This is the position of several scholars, most notably T. S. Rukmani, for whom this commentary cannot date from before the fourteenth century. Central
† to their argument is the fact that the ninth-century

Shankaracharya flatly rejects the "stoppage of the turnings of thought" of *Yoga Sutra* 1.2 as a means to release from suffering existence. Trevor Leggett, the editor and translator of the "Exposition," offers several counterarguments to this position. As Leggett notes, this †
commentator takes many of the same positions and uses much of the same philosophical terminology as those of the ninth-century figure who authored the commentary on the *Bhagavad Gita* and other works. This commentator's argument *against* the Samkhya Dualism of the *Yoga Sutra* and Vyasa's commentary is also typical of the great Shankara's Advaita Vedanta position. Most importantly, his assertion that there is †
only one Purusha—and that that Purusha is God, Ishvara, who dwells in everything, but whose power of illusion is the cause of suffering for the ignorant—is Leggett's proof that this was the work of the great ninth-century teacher. In effect, Shankara devotes the †
longest passages of his "Exposition" to demonstrating that Patanjali's Ishvara is none other than the supreme being who created the universe and who is the object of Hindu devotion.

The sole classical commentator capable of holding his own with Shankara in terms of erudition, debating skills, and originality was the circa 950 CE Vachaspati Mishra, whose given name speaks volumes on who and what he was: Vachaspati means "Talk-Meister." The author of eight major works covering all of the †
major philosophical systems, Vachaspati Mishra was something of an intellectual diva, capable "of advocat-

ing each of them even when their standpoints were at variance with one another."[5] So it is that we see him
† attacking the possibility of direct yogic perception in a commentary on Nyaya philosophy, and treating the same with complete seriousness in his commentary on the *Yoga Sutra*. That work, titled the *Tattvavaisharadi* ("Expert Guide to the True Principles"), is considered to be the most learned, balanced, and comprehensive of all *Yoga Sutra* commentaries. That being said, Vachaspati Mishra did not regard the *Yoga Sutra* to be the sole authority on Yoga philosophy. Quoting a work titled the *Yogi Yajnavalkyasmriti* ("Tradition of Yogi Ya-
† jnavalkya"), he inferred that Hiranyagarbha's Yoga system may have preceded Patanjali's. Elsewhere, in his commentary on the *Vedantasutras*, he expressed doubt that the axioms of Vedanta could ever challenge the authority of these two Yoga systems. As we will see, history proved him to be incorrect on this count.

Vachaspati Mishra's work was the main inspiration for King Bhoja's eleventh-century *Rajamartandavritti* ("Royal Sun Commentary"), quoted above on the subject of the three-in-one Patanjali. Unlike every other major commentator on the *Yoga Sutra*, Bhoja wholeheartedly embraced Yoga philosophy, devoting the
† final portion of his commentary to a Samkhya-Yoga refutation of every other school's position on the nature of Purusha. We have already seen that Bhoja did not hesitate to compare himself to Patanjali in terms of commentarial prowess. In the final words of his commentary, he praises himself yet again, speaking of

other kings who are "prostrate at his feet in acts of ser- †
vice and salutation." This may not have been an idle
boast. The illustrious ruler of the kingdom of Malwa
in west central India, he is one of the rare classical
commentators about whom we have some biographical data. An enlightened despot, Bhoja was also a great †
military strategist who succeeded in driving back, if
only for a time, Mahmud of Ghazni, the notorious Af-
ghan invader who was the scourge of western India in
the opening decades of the eleventh century. He was
also an exemplary patron of the arts and the innovator
of a massive public works project involving the dam-
ming of two rivers for the creation of the massive
250-square-mile Bhojpur Lake.

The centuries separating Vachaspati Mishra and
Bhoja were the *Yoga Sutra*'s glory days. This was the period during which Patanjali's work was most widely
quoted and enjoyed its greatest prestige, from Kashmir to Indonesia to Central Asia. But by the sixteenth
century, the time of Vijnanabhiksu, the *Yoga Sutra*'s
last great commentator, things had changed. On the
one hand, a new religio-philosophical paradigm had
been forged between the theism of the Puranas and
Vedanta philosophy. On the other, brahmin orthodoxy had, in the face of the onslaught of Islam in the
northern part of the subcontinent, hardened with respect to all "non-Vedic" traditions, including Yoga.

Vijnanabhiksu was the author of two commentaries—the *Yogavarttika* ("Explanation of Yoga") and the
Yogasarasamgraha ("Short Statement on the Essence

of Yoga"). Like Shankara, Vijnanabhikshu was a Vedanta philosopher; however, unlike Shankara, he was not an Advaita Vedanta philosopher. Rather than taking a Nondualist stance, his was what has been termed "Qualified Nondualism" (Vishishtadvaita). For Vijnanabhikshu, this meant that while the union of each individual Purusha with the divine could be realized psychologically, the two would always remain separate on a metaphysical level, in the same way that Purusha and Prakriti were always metaphysically separate.

Most important for the history of *Yoga Sutra* commentary, however, was Vijnanabhikshu's position on Ishvara. While earlier commentators (with the exception of Shankara, if his "Exposition" had in fact been written in the ninth century) had refused to allow that Patanjali's Ishvara could be construed as the divine creator of the universe, Vijnanabhikshu saw matters differently. This is not to say that he was the originator of the ideas he was expounding: although he wrote as a philosopher (and perhaps a yoga practitioner, as Rukmani has maintained), he was also a man of his times, and by the sixteenth century the Hindu world had radically changed. In fact, it had been changing since the time of the *Bhagavad Gita* and the Puranas, which defined Yoga not as the "stoppage of the turnings of thought," but rather as union with God.

About a dozen Puranas, dating from the fourth to fourteenth centuries, contain one or more chapters on Yoga. Not one of these gives a comprehensive account of the *Yoga Sutra* or its philosophical system, and al-

though five Puranas provide long lists of yoga gurus †
and disciples, Patanjali's name is conspicuously absent
from all of them. Instead, one finds in them the names
of mainly Vedic and Upanishadic sages—but also
those of Kapila, the legendary revealer of the Samkhya
system, and Hiranyagarbha, whom the *Mahabharata*
had identified as the founder of the Yoga system.
Across all of the Puranas, only a handful of verses from †
the *Yoga Sutra* are quoted—and most of these inaccu-
rately. Only five—the *Agni*, *Shiva*, *Linga*, *Kurma*, and †
Markandeya—provide even a paraphrase of the *Yoga
Sutra's* definition of Yoga. About half mention the
eight-part practice, the others focusing instead on the
six-part practice (shadangayoga) of the *Maitri Upanishad*, the "three yogas" of the *Bhagavad Gita*, as well as
Pashupata Yoga, Hatha Yoga, Tantric Yoga, the healing
properties of yoga, and so forth. As for the seven Pura- †
nas that do discuss the eight-part practice, none frame
it within the context of Samkhya-Yoga philosophy,
and only the *Shiva* acknowledges the *Yoga Shastra* †
(which may not be the same work as the *Yoga Sutra*) as
its source. None respect the *Yoga Sutra's* account of
Ishvara, but rather speak of Yoga as union with a supreme creator god, identified with both the Brahman
of Vedanta philosophy and either Vishnu, Shiva, or
Devi, the three supreme deities of Hindu theism.

In reading these authoritative works on medieval
Hinduism, one comes away with the impression that
their authors were either unaware of the *Yoga Sutra*
as an independent tradition, or that they were self-

consciously censoring Patanjali from their Puranic systems—which were, after all, grounded in the power of an omnipotent God to offer grace and salvation to all His (or Her) devotees. Indeed, this is the principal use the Puranas make of the eight-part practice: as a means to meditating on God in one's own heart and realizing union with Him. Most critical Yoga scholars agree that the eight-part practice was a preexisting independent tradition that Patanjali adapted into his *Yoga Sutra*. While it cannot be known whether the *Mahabharata*'s teachings on Yoga were earlier or later than the *Yoga Sutra*, the fact is that the *Mahabharata*'s twelfth book does briefly mention the eight-part practice. This being the case, it is possible that the compilers of the Puranas—the earliest of which may have predated the *Yoga Sutra* but postdated the *Mahabharata*—were entirely unaware of Patanjali and his Dualist Samkhya-based Yoga system. As we will see in later chapters, virtually every modern-day yoga guru beginning with Swami Vivekananda has followed the lead of the Puranas, rather than that of the *Yoga Sutra*, in their interpretation of the eight-part practice. In other words, they have fundamentally misconstrued what they consider to be the very heart of Patanjali's system.

Clearly influenced by the Puranic traditions, Vijnanabhikshu affirmed that even if the goal of Yoga practice were the isolation of the Person from Matter, this did not preclude the fact that beyond each individual spirit there was God, the supreme Self and the creator of all, transcending all. For this reason, he chose to view Ishvara as the twenty-sixth principle, higher even than the multiple Purushas identified as the twenty-fifth and highest principle in classical Samkhya. This assertion, already found in the *Mahabharata*'s twelfth book and several later works, is nowhere present in earlier *Yoga Sutra* commentary. †

Patanjali and Vyasa had presented Ishvara as an object of meditation, a means to the end of the stoppage of the turnings of thought and the ultimate goal of the isolation of the individual Person from universal Matter. In Vedanta philosophy and Puranic theism however, God became both the alpha and the omega of meditation: the practitioner, by meditating on Him (or Her) in his heart, realizes the innate and eternal identity of his individual self with the universal Self. A number of works betray the transition, from Samkhya Dualism to Vedanta Nondualism, and from the Ishvara of Patanjali's system to the universal Self of Vedanta. One of these was the *Agni Purana,* which fused † the two into a principle called Brahman-Ishvara, and identified samadhi as the individual soul's union with that principle. Another was the circa 1340 *Sarvadarshanasamgraha* ("Compendium of All the Systems"), the last great philosophical work to truly defend Patanjali's system. Yet in doing so, its author, Sayana Madhava, a royal minister from the south Indian Vijayanagara kingdom, nonetheless betrayed the erosion of the position of the *Yoga Sutra* with respect to both Vedanta and other Yoga systems. Even as he championed what he termed the "Patanjali Darshana," ranking it higher than all of the sixteen systems he surveyed with the exception of Vedanta, Madhava tailored Yoga philosophy to conform to Vedanta doctrines. So it is that while he supported Vyasa's emphatic reading of *Yoga Sutra* 1.2—that Yoga was to be defined as samadhi and *not* union—he nonetheless argued, from the precedent of a tenth- to twelfth-century south Indian work titled the *Yoga Yajnavalkya* ("Yajnavalkya's Yoga"), that

† the word samadhi itself could also be read to mean "union." In the same spirit of devotion that was the hallmark of medieval Hindu theism, but not of Patan-

† jali's system, Madhava equated Ishvara with Krishna, whom he identified as the transcendent twenty-sixth

† principle. Elsewhere, he also introduced several elements of Tantric and Hatha Yoga into his account of Patanjali's system, including the use of specifically tantric mantras, discussions of yogic physiology, and techniques of breath control.

Vijnanabhiksu had no compunctions about adding the supreme category of Ishvara to the standard

† Samkhyan system, because for him, the atheism of Samkhya was a "mere hyperbolic assertion," a "concession to current views," given the fact that by his time "Samkhya doctrine [had] been devoured by the sun of time and only a tiny crescent moon of [its form of] knowledge [was] still visible."⁶ And so it was that by the sixteenth century, devotional Hinduism, which equated the universal Self of Vedanta philosophy with a personal God, had collapsed nearly every philosophical system into its perfect theological crystal. In a com-

plete reversal of Patanjali's and Vyasa's original positions, the Ishvara of the *Yoga Sutra* had come to be   †
equated with the Krishna of the *Bhagavad Gita*.

During the same period that it was being eclipsed
by the theistic Yoga systems of the Puranas, the *Yoga
Sutra* was being openly attacked on another front.
Here I am speaking of commentators on the compen-
dia of orthodox Hindu law known as the Smritis.
Some of the Smritis date from the time of the Hindu
epics, and as such predate the Puranas, which also
quote from them extensively. Toward the end of the
tenth century, a series of invasions by Muslim warlords
and empire builders provoked a backlash among the
north Indian brahmin orthodoxy against all that was
not "Vedic" in Hindu theory and practice. Much of
the ideology of this project of hieratic entrenchment
may be found in commentaries written on the Smritis
during this period.

Most interesting is the position taken by Lakshmidhara, a mid-twelfth-century royal minister, judge, and
legal scholar from the kingdom of Kanauj in India's
Gangetic heartland, and author of the massive *Krityakalpataru* ("The Wish-Fulfilling Tree of Sacred Duty").
A "great encyclopedic construction of the 'Hindu way   †
of life,'" this digest of Hindu law was compiled precisely, according to Sheldon Pollack, as an orthodox
Hindu reaction to repeated Islamic encroachments
into the Indian subcontinent. Lakshmidhara's is mainly
an *argumentum ex silentio*. In his six chapters on Yoga,
he quotes over five hundred verses from the *Bhagavad*

Gita, the *Mahabharata*'s twelfth book, six Puranas, and several other works, but only two verses from the *Yoga Sutra*. While he does acknowledge Patanjali as the source for his definition of Yoga, he nonetheless attributes the eight-part practice to the *Mahabharata*. In fact, a verse from the *Mahabharata*'s twelfth book harks back to Vedic sages who "described Yoga as eightfold," and long passages from the same book encapsulate many of the basic tenets of Yoga philosophy, obviating the need for Lakshmidhara to refer to Patanjali as his standard reference.

In addition to scripture, orthodox commentators like Lakshmidhara also favored works attributed to Yajnavalkya over Patanjali's *Yoga Sutra* as their authorized source on Yoga. Several works, including the "Tradition of Yogi Yajnavalkya" and "Yajnavalkya's Yoga," were attributed to this latter figure who, because his was the same name as that of an Upanishadic sage, was considered to be an ancient authority. For Advaita Vedanta commentators, the *Yoga Vasistha*, a tenth- to thirteenth-century work attributed to the Vedic sage Vasistha, became the reference of choice in matters of Yoga philosophy. Others, as we have seen, favored the divine Hiranyagarbha as their default founder of the Yoga system. Without such *titres de noblesse*, Patanjali and his work were discredited as inauthentic. On the basis of these data, we can see that by the twelfth century, Patanjali's system had been caught in a pincer movement of sorts, rejected by orthodox brahmins for being beyond the pale of the Vedas and by the burgeoning ranks of Hindu devotees of gods like Krishna, Vishnu, and Shiva for being nondevotional.

In comparing the commentarial tradition to the process of judicial review in chapter 1, I suggested that through changing philosophical and real-world contexts, gradual shifts in the perceived meanings of concepts could gradually alter the global understanding of a philosophical work, sometimes beyond recognition. This was the effect that Vijnanabhikshu's theistic reading of Ishvara had on *Yoga Sutra* commentary. Following him, there would be very few original commentaries on Patanjali's work, and what rare commentaries there were tended only to accentuate the trend he had initiated, further overwriting its Samkhya-Yoga material with a Vedanta-based devotional gloss. When devotion to an omnipotent personal God or Goddess was sufficient to free humans from suffering existence, what need was there for Yoga practice, for the difficult task of clarifying the mind-stuff and meditating on the individual Purusha's intrinsic isolation from Prakriti? By Vijnanabhikshu's time, Vedanta-based Hindu devotion had rendered Yoga philosophy irrelevant. This is not to say that Vijnanabhikshu single-handedly brought about the death of Yoga philosophy, which had been in decline for several centuries before him: he simply made it official. For the following three centuries, nearly all of India would be a Yoga desert.

†

Henry Thomas Colebrooke and the Western "Discovery" of the *Yoga Sutra*

Unlike the *Yoga Sutra*'s classical commentators, relatively few modern-day Yoga scholars are either Indian or Hindu. Over the past one hundred years in particular, foreign scholars have generated the bulk of the new theoretical perspectives on Patanjali's work. The story of how foreign scholars backed into—or, more properly speaking, revived—the *Yoga Sutra*'s ancient traditions is as fascinating and improbable as the strange two-hundred-year clash of cultures commonly known as the British Raj.

Some time in the late eighteenth century, some of the British who had been effectively controlling much of the rich territory of Bengal for several decades were beginning to realize that foreign occupation could have unanticipated consequences. Things had begun swimmingly enough on June 23, 1757, when, in the midst of the Seven Years' War, an army of three thousand men led by the British colonel Robert Clive had defeated the Nawab of Bengal at the Battle of Plassey.

This was a turning point in the formation of what would become the British Empire in India, but at this point, England's influence in India was indirect. Acting as a proxy for the Crown in eighteenth-century India was the British East India Company, a trading consortium that was but one among several rival companies vying for control over the vast resources and markets of Asia. In Bengal, the Company's greatest competitor was its French homologue, the French East India Company.

Nearly a year to the day prior to the Battle of Plassey, the same Nawab of Bengal had captured Fort William, the Company's fortified headquarters near the mouth of the Hooghly River, and allegedly caused the death by suffocation of 123 of its British defenders in the June heat of the "Black Hole of Calcutta." So it was that the victory at Plassey was doubly sweet for the British, because with its defeat of the Nawab, it had also defeated the French who had sided with him. The Nawab was   †
forced to make major concessions, with the coup de grâce coming in 1765 when the Mughal emperor in Delhi transferred the *diwani*—the right of civil and revenue administration—over the eastern provinces of Bengal, Bihar, and Orissa from the Nawab to the Company. Then in 1772, the Company's governor, Warren Hastings, chose Calcutta (today known as Kolkata), at the time little more than a swampy village of mud huts, to be its capital.

The Company was first and foremost a commercial   †
enterprise, whose raison d'être was to maximize profits

for its shareholders. To this end it recruited very young men from Britain (their average age was sixteen) to oversee its massive plantations and factory operations, which were run by local subcontractors. Many of these young men turned out to be self-serving adventurers, with those who succeeded returning to Britain some years later with vast personal fortunes. Preemployment training was not a high priority in those early years: in order to be hired, a certificate in accounting was sufficient, and all other training—in local languages, business administration, and so forth—was of the on-the-job variety. However, the civil administration of the Company's territories included the administration of justice, and it was here that a clause in Hastings's Judicial Plan of 1772 gave rise, albeit indirectly, to the British "discovery" of the *Yoga Sutra*. That clause proclaimed that rather than imposing British common law upon the people of Bengal, which would have been terribly unfair albeit not without precedent, Hindus would be judged according to Hindu law and Muslims according to Islamic law. Unfortunately for the British, they had no knowledge of either.

Islamic law was a relatively easy fix; since it had been the law of the Mughal Empire in India for hundreds of years, its canon, even if it was written in Arabic and Persian, was at least identifiable. Hindu law, however, was unknown territory. What were the codes of Hindu law, and where were they to be found? From the outset, it was determined that the sources of Hindu law could more easily be ferreted out of Hindu law books than by observing and cataloging contemporary local customs. As the British were made to understand by the brahmin religious specialists known as pandits, the canon of Hindu law had been written in the language known as Sanskrit, the "perfected" language of their scriptures. And so it was that in the final decades of the eighteenth century an unanticipated consequence of the British occupation of Bengal was the urgent necessity to learn Sanskrit, one of the most confoundedly difficult languages on the planet.

In the earliest phases of their learning curve, the British were entirely dependent on the Bengali pandits, whom Hastings actively recruited for unlocking the mysteries of all things Hindu. They identified the primary teachings of sacred Hindu law (Dharma Shastra, shortened to "the Shaster" by the British), and they translated them and interpreted their meaning to the British, generally through the medium of Bengali, the spoken language of the territory. By 1776, Hastings's Judicial Plan had begun to show results, in the form of Nathaniel Brassey Halhed's English-language rendering of the Hindu law code, published under the title *A Code of Gentoo Laws*. This quickly proved insufficient however, and so in 1788 William Jones proposed a second and far more substantial work. In the end, the completion of that task would fall to a Sanskritist named Henry Thomas Colebrooke. Together with Jones, Colebrooke was a founding father of British Orientalism, and their discovery and gradual mastery of many of the wonders of the Sanskrit language and its massive literary tradition may be viewed as a direct and happy side effect of Hastings's Judicial Plan.

Jones, a distant ancestor of Lady Di, had first arrived in Kolkata in March of 1783. Sent there to serve as justice on the Supreme Court of Bengal, he was an unusual judge inasmuch as he had, long prior to studying law in the early 1770s, distinguished himself as a specialist of ancient languages. Soon after taking his

† post, however, Jones began to suspect that the local pandits had perhaps been snookering him and his colleagues, making up legal rulings on the fly or to their own advantage even as they claimed to be quoting chapter and verse of the Shaster. He said as much in a letter written to Hastings in 1784, but his formal project for a *Digest of Hindu Law on Contracts and Successions* would not be submitted until 1788. Unlike the 1776 *Code*, the digest would be an "in-house" translation, fully prepared this time by British Sanskritists.

Jones and his fellow members of the Asiatic Society unabashedly referred to themselves as Orientalists, a term that has been associated, in the wake of Edward Said's groundbreaking *Orientalism* (1978), with imperial domination, colonial projects, and the notions of European superiority epitomized in Kipling's "White man's burden." Such charges are altogether justifiable for the Anglicists, whose theories of "Oriental irrationality" came to dominate Britain's increasingly imperialist policies toward India from the 1830s onward. However, as Rosane Rocher and others have demonstrated, the attitude of the Orientalists, the Company's scholar-administrators of the early decades of the nineteenth century, was altogether different. Like Jones, as Rocher notes, "many of the early aficionados of Indian culture... had had a classical education. They knew from the accounts of India given in the Greek and Latin classics, of the existence in ancient times of what the Greeks called gymnosophists, or naked philosophers. They knew that Indian culture had a long and distinguished history."[1]

The British Orientalist legacy has continued to burn most brightly in the academic discipline of Indology, which takes as its primary object the literary treasury of Sanskrit, the classical language of one of the world's great civilizations, with privilege of place given to its religious and philosophical canons. This emphasis is reflected in the earliest publications of the fledgling Asiatic Society, which included, in addition to translations of the ancient Indian law books, Sir Charles Wilkins's 1785 English-language *Bhagavad Gita*. It is here that one finds the earliest European reference to the *Yoga Sutra*: in a footnote, Wilkins mentions "a metaphysical work called *Patanjal*."[2] In addition to translations such as these, the Society's members also began to publish independent studies treating various aspects of Indian geography, history, philosophy, religion, culture, and science in *Asiatic Researches*, which commenced publication in 1788.

Volume eight of that journal, published in 1805, contains the earliest authoritative western study of the Vedas, authored by Colebrooke. The son of a baronet

† who had fallen on hard times, Colebrooke had sailed to Bengal in 1782 to take a position in the Company. It was during his early years of service, as he gradually climbed the Company ladder at several backcountry postings, that he began to study Sanskrit. Quickly drawn into the intimate circle of the British Orientalists, he soon became active in the Asiatic Society, which had been

† founded by Jones in 1784. A year later, he was appointed district magistrate at Mirzapur, an important commercial town located a short way up the Ganges River from the holy city of Varanasi (then known as Benares). In this period he completed the project Jones had proposed in 1788, a monumental four-volume digest of indigenous Hindu and Islamic law, which was eventually published in 1798. A landmark year for him was 1805, when he saw the publication of both his study on the religion of the Vedas and the first volume of his grammar of the Sanskrit language, as well as his appointment to the position of honorary professor of Hindu law and Sanskrit at the recently founded College of Fort William, situated in the heart of the Company's still humble trading port of Calcutta.

Rightly hailed by Friedrich Max Müller as the founder and father of Sanskrit scholarship in Europe, Colebrooke maintained an active role at Fort William until his return to England in 1814. It was there that in 1823 he authored a groundbreaking essay on Samkhya and Yoga philosophy as the first installment in a three-part survey of the six systems, titled "On the Philosophy of the Hindus." This, the "first contact" between a

European Sanskritist and the Sanskrit-language tradition of the *Yoga Sutra*, Colebrooke's reading of Patanjali's work effectively cut the *Yoga Sutra* free from its Indian moorings—from which it has been drifting ever since.

Colebrooke's 1823–27 study is a model of economy †
and clarity, remarkably comprehensive in both scope and depth. In it Colebrooke shows himself to be highly sympathetic to Indian philosophy, as he presents the systems in an objective and evenhanded way. With a single exception, he shows great respect for his subject, allowing in some cases that India may have been the †
source of several ancient Greek philosophical doctrines. This was but one aspect of his broader vision of the history of human thought. At his inaugural speech †
to the Royal Asiatic Society of Great Britain and Ireland, presented on March 15, 1823, he flatly asserted that all of civilization had its origin in Asia, for which the West owed that continent a debt of gratitude. Here he was simply reiterating the position of the British Orientalists, and while it is true that the voices of the Orientalists would soon be drowned out by those of the jingoist Anglicists who won the day in terms of British policy, their appreciation of all things Indian would in later decades be elevated to a matter of faith among the European Romantics, who viewed ancient India as the lost paradise of humanity and the fountainhead of all human wisdom and spirituality. This rosy vision would gradually morph into a more muscular gospel of Indian exceptionalism, whose themes may

be found in the writings and teachings of the Theosophical Society, Swami Vivekananda, and modern-day Hindu nationalists.

Colebrooke's study of the six systems appears to have been exclusively based on his own exhaustive study of Sanskrit-language manuscripts, undertaken without recourse to the Indian pandits. (As we will see, his personal collection of such manuscripts was legendary.) Colebrooke's 1823 study, far shorter than those he would later publish on Nyaya-Vaisheshika and Mimamsa-Vedanta, is not titled "Samkhya-Yoga," but rather simply "Samkhya." Colebrooke explains the omission of "Yoga" from his title by arguing that Yoga is but a variant form of Samkhya philosophy. In this, he is simply following the commentarial tradition mentioned in the last chapter, which speaks of Yoga as simply "Samkhya with Ishvara" (seshvara samkhya)—with Ishvara, the "Master" of Yoga, taken by many commentators to mean "God." In Colebrooke's words,

the one school (PATANJALI'S) recognising GOD, is therefore denominated theistical (*Séśwara sánc'hya*). The other (CAPILA'S) is atheistical (*Niríśwara sánc'hya*). . . . Such is the essential and characteristic difference of CAPILA'S and PATANJALI'S, the atheistical and deistical, *Sánc'hyas*. In less momentous matters they differ, not upon points of doctrine, but in the degree in which the exterior exercises, or abstruse reasoning and study, are weighed upon, as requisite preparations of absorbed contemplation.[3]

Colebrooke dwells but little on the distinctiveness of the Yoga school, devoting fewer than five pages of his study (compared to the twenty-eight given over to Samkhya) to its doctrines, commentators, and traditions. One might attribute this seemingly dismissive attitude as simply flowing from the fact that the *Yoga Sutra* is often called an "interpretation of Samkhya" (samkhya-pravachana) in its manuscript colophons. Noting this, Colebrooke chose to focus on the primary source of Samkhya philosophy, the *Samkhya Karika*, which he attributed to Kapila, the legendary founder of the school, rather than to its author Ishvara Krishna. But Colebrooke's treatment of Yoga philosophy goes beyond the dismissive, as his few salient observations on it make clear:

> Besides the *Sánc'hya* of CAPILA and his followers, † another system, bearing the same denomination, but more usually termed the *Yóga-śástra* or *Yóga-sútra*... is ascribed to a mythological being, PATANJALI. . . . An ancient commentary on this fanatical work is ... entitled *Pátanjala-bháshya*. It is attributed to VÉDA-VYÁSA. . . . The tenets of the two schools of the *Sánc'hya* are on many, not to say on most, points, that are treated in both, the same; differing however upon one, which is the most important of all: the proof of existence of supreme GOD . . . PATANJALI'S *Yoga-śástra* is occupied

with devotional exercise and mental abstraction, subduing body and mind: CAPILA is more engaged with investigation of principles and reasoning upon them. One is more mystic and fanatical. The other makes a nearer approach to philosophical disquisition, however mistaken in its conclusions.[4]

While it is clear that Colebrooke is not enthralled by the precepts of Samkhya philosophy, he nonetheless appreciates it as philosophy. The same holds for his accounts of the four other schools, for which his general attitude of respect far outweighs the occasional disparaging remark. In his entire study of the six systems, the sole instances in which Colebrooke uses the word "fanatical" or employs any other such loaded term are those quoted here on the topic of the *Yoga Sutra*. His choice of words would continue to resonate throughout much of the nineteenth century. In his 1855 translation of the *Bhagavad Gita*, the British Orientalist J. Cockburn Thomson applauded the sobriety of Krishna's teaching, saying "in this there is no fanaticism, as there may be in the asceticism taught by Patanjali."[5] The American Orientalist Fitzedward Hall was of a rather stronger opinion, as evidenced in an 1859 publication with the regrettable title *A Contribution towards an Index to the Bibliography of the Indian Philosophical Systems*. Note, however, that Hall's criticism is directed against the entire canon of Yoga philosophy, which extended well beyond the purview of the *Yoga Sutra* and its commentaries:

As few of the twenty-eight Yoga works which have
fallen under my inspection are at present read, so,
one may hope, few will ever again be read, either in
this country or by curious enquirers in Europe. If
we exclude the immundities [*sic*] of the *Tantras*
and of the *Káma-sastra*, Hindu thought was never
more unworthily engaged than in digesting into an
economy the fanatical vagaries of theocracy.[6]

Rajendralal Mitra, who quotes Hall in the introduction to his 1883 translation of the *Yoga Sutra*, next
makes a move that would be widely followed for much
of the following century: he separates Yoga philosophy
from India's yogis, placing the onus of the fanatical not
on the *Yoga Sutra* itself but rather on its abuse by its
supposed practitioners: "In judging, however, of the
nature of Patanjali's doctrine it is unfair to associate it
with the vagaries of fanatical, deluded mendicants, or
with the modifications and adaptations which it has
undergone in the hands of the Tantrics and the Pura-
nics."[7] So, too, in 1889, Romesh Chunder Dutt would
write that "the philosophy of the Yoga system has been
completely lost sight of, and the system has degenerated into cruel and indecent Tantrika rites, or into the
impostures and superstitions of the so-called Yogins of
the present day."[8] Max Müller would follow suit in his
1899 study, *The Six Systems of Indian Philosophy*, referring to Hatha or Kriya Yoga as "pathological," with its
modern-day proponents, the "modern Yogins or Ma-
hatmans" as "frauds." It may well be that Colebrooke

also had India's yogis in mind when he dismissed Patanjali's system as fanatical, since in one of his longer discussions of the *Yoga Sutra* he explicitly linked their practices to its doctrines:

† The notion, that . . . transcendent power is attainable by man in this life, is not peculiar to the *Sánc'hya* sect: it is generally prevalent among the Hindus, and amounts to a belief in magic. A *Yógí*, imagined to have acquired such faculties, is, to vulgar apprehension, a sorcerer, and is so represented in many a drama and popular tale. One of the four chapters of PATANJALI'S *Yóga-śástra* (the third), relates almost exclusively to this subject. . . . It is full of directions for bodily and mental exercises, consisting of intensely profound meditation on special topics, accompanied by suppression of the breath and restraint of the senses, while steadily maintaining prescribed postures. By such exercises, the adept acquires the knowledge of every thing past and future, remote or hidden; gains the strength of an elephant, the courage of a lion, and the swiftness of the wind; flies in the air, floats in water, dives into the earth, contemplates all worlds with one glance, and performs other strange feats.[9]

While the *Yoga Sutra* has been called many things by many people, fanatical is not the first that comes to mind. Why, then, so much sound and fury regarding India's fanatical yogis? Most of us in the twenty-first century view India's traditional yogis as peaceful, forest-dwelling sages, living in harmony with bird and beast and passing their days and nights in rapt meditation on the Absolute within. This is how the forest sages are portrayed in India's ancient literature, and in that timeless land of unchanging tradition, that is how they have remained. While these persons are nowhere referred to as yogis in the ancient literature, the *Yoga Sutra* and other works from the early centuries CE (the Hindu *Bhagavad Gita* and *Maitri Upanishad* and the Buddhist *Milindapanha*, for example) do; in them, for the first time, practitioners of the various types of Yoga they espouse are called "yogis."

How interesting, then, that not a single nineteenth-century account, by either Europeans or Indians—or by the yogis themselves—portrays them as peaceful ascetics practicing meditation *pace* the *Yoga Sutra*. Instead, the overwhelming majority of accounts from the sixteenth century onward depict yogis as either beggars or ragtag mercenary fighters. On the first † count, a multitude of eyewitness reports speak of marauding bands of yogis behaving like shake-down artists, mobbing entrances to temples, pilgrimage sites, and public markets, staging freak shows (the "mango trick" and infamous beds of nails), or simply creating a ruckus until harassed merchants would pay them off simply to go away and hector someone else. On the † second, they were viewed in much the same way as the modern-day Taliban, as part religious fanatic and part terrorist, fighting gangs of warriors known to poison their enemies or cut their throats to drink their warm blood.

This was the Europeans' outsider view of India's yogis. But what do insider Indian accounts tell us? In the medieval scriptures known as the Tantras, the term *yogi* most often referred to a Tantric specialist who had received various initiations that empowered him to practice Tantric Yoga, which involved, among other things, the power to take over other people's bodies and to consort sexually with ferocious female predators called Yoginis. Woe to the uninitiated who might attempt the same, however: the Yoginis would tear them apart and eat them, which certainly puts a new wrinkle on the "Yogini" Gonika of Iyengar mythology. In much of India's medieval and modern fantasy and adventure literature, the evil villain is called a yogi, and even today, when naughty children will not go to sleep at night, their parents will threaten that "the yogi will come and take you away." Regarded with dread and fear by the Hindu populace, India's yogis assert that their supernatural powers flow directly from empowering initiations and extraordinary feats of self-discipline. Yet while these powers often align with those described in the *Yoga Sutra*'s third chapter, very few Tantric schools or sects have ever explicitly linked their theory or practice to Patanjali's legacy.

Having said this, there is likely more behind Colebrooke's references to the "fanatical" than simply a philosophical distaste for a profligate lifestyle. Here, a nineteenth-century collection of legends, compiled by a yogi belonging to the powerful order known as the Kanphata Yogis ("Split-Eared Yogis") or Nath Yogis ("Yogi Lords"), is highly instructive. In it, we read of a historical figure named Mastnath (the "Lord of Intoxication") whose many supernatural feats included calling down plagues on villages that refused to offer him alms, turning camel bones into gold, and raising a besieged prince named Man Singh to the throne of the kingdom of Marwar in the modern-day western Indian state of Rajasthan. In this last case Mastnath produced a series of miracles culminating in the sudden death of the young prince's rival, in return for which the Yogi Lords were granted a network of temples and monasteries throughout the kingdom. James Tod, a Company agent, also chronicled the same tumultuous chapter in Marwar history, but he put an altogether different spin on things. According to his 1820 report, Mastnath's "miracle" was the result of "a dose of poison." In other words, a Yogi Lord had infiltrated the rival camp and assassinated its leader. Tod's rage at the yogis' subterfuge is palpable:

> During the few years he held the keys of his master's conscience, which were conveniently employed to unlock the treasury, he erected no less than eighty-four mandirs [temples] . . . with monasteries adjoining them, for his well-fed lazy chelas [disciples]. . . . This [Cardinal] Wolsely of Marudes [the western desert] exercised his hourly-increasing

power to the disgust and alienation of all but the infatuated prince.[10]

Here, Tod's righteous indignation at this yogi pontiff of the western desert reminds us of Hall's diatribe against the "fanatical vagaries of theocracy" in his assessment of Yoga philosophy. To be sure, the British viewed the yogis, with their beggary, Tantric sorcery, and debauched sexuality as morally repugnant—but there was more going on here than first meets the eye. The case of Marwar is especially instructive, because the historical record shows that Man Singh's rival Bhim Singh—whose sudden death, perhaps by poisoning, opened the way for the young prince to take the throne in 1803—was the very man whom the Company had been backing. In other words, the all-powerful Company had been outmaneuvered by a homicidal band of yogis, who were now ruling a vast territory of western India by proxy. Shades of Mullah Omar.

This was not an isolated incident. Time and again, from the late eighteenth well into the nineteenth century, a variety of mendicant orders—variously called Yogis, Gosains, Fakirs, or Sanyasis by the British, who had difficulty distinguishing between them—stymied Company designs through guerilla warfare, shrewd political maneuvering, and commercial savvy. Then, too, there were the yogis' sheer numbers. Already in the middle of the seventeenth century, the French merchant Jean-Baptiste Tavernier had estimated there to be some two million of them in India. Tavernier also noted that many of these were armed, and as Dirk Kolff has shown, the bulk of the eighteenth- and early nineteenth-century north Indian military labor market was made up of armed ascetics, with a single religious order (the Nagas) alone counting for some 300,000 warriors. Throughout the final three decades of the eighteenth century, the Company had found itself pitted against a yogi insurgency in Bengal, which came to be known as the "Sanyasi and Fakir Rebellion."

For much of the eighteenth century, the Company also found itself countered by the yogis in its attempts to regulate and exploit north Indian commerce. Here, groups that Christopher Bayly has called "corporations of Hindu ascetics and mercenaries" leveraged their status as "holy men" to transform pilgrimage routes into trading networks. The British may well have viewed them as marauders and robbers, but the fact remained that the yogis had, by the 1780s, become the dominant moneylenders, property owners, and pillars of the merchant communities of Allahabad, Varanasi, and Mirzapur, the principal trading centers of the rich Gangetic plain.

In the years around 1795, Colebrooke was working in the Company's employ at Mirzapur. By now an accomplished Sanskritist, he no doubt traveled downriver to the holy city of Varanasi—which was at that time in the midst of an economic and religious renaissance—for access to Sanskrit manuscripts to add to his growing collection. There, the powerful western Indian trading houses of Sindhia and Holkar were patrons of a conservative brand of Hinduism, which they fostered by establishing brahmin "colleges" for the training of pandits. The policy worked so well that by † 1810 there were more than 40,000 brahmins living on charity there, accounting for nearly 20 percent of the city's total population. But the yogis were also an important presence. The 1827–28 census data indicate † that "Hindu Fakirs"—that is, yogis—made up 4 percent of the city's *entire* population, but this only referred to members of the mendicant orders living there permanently, as opposed to the hordes of itinerant yogis that were constantly passing through.

With the Sanyasi and Fakir Rebellion a recent memory in Bengal, and the highly visible presence of wandering ascetics in Varanasi and Mirzapur a contemporary reality, Colebrooke would have been altogether familiar with the yogis and their "fanatical" ways. Given that none of these yogis had any interest whatsoever in the philosophical and meditative teachings of the *Yoga Sutra*, one must ask whether there remained some other group from Indian society that had continued to cultivate its ancient traditions. The obvious candidate would have been the pandits, the masters of the brahmin colleges—of Varanasi in the Gangetic heartland and Nadia in Bengal—whose stock in trade was the transmission of traditional Hindu knowledge from generation to generation. A precious data source for the early nineteenth century are the writings of William Ward, a British Baptist clergyman who for several decades ran the important Serampore Mission a short distance upriver from Kolkata. While he had no training as a Sanskritist and adopted a missionary attitude toward Bengal's "heathen" population, which he sought to convert with very limited success, Ward is noteworthy for having written an early survey of Hinduism titled *View of the History, Literature, and Religion of the Hindoos*. First published in 1810, his study included a long descriptive account of Patanjali's system, which he ostensibly based on Bhoja's commentary on the *Yoga Sutra*. †

At the end of Ward's expanded 1820 third edition of the work is a long chapter on the state of traditional brahmanic education in the various colleges and monasteries of Varanasi. In it, he provides detailed lists for the year 1817 of the "convents of ascetics, at Benares" where the various branches of traditional learning were taught. For Vedic study, no fewer than forty-eight establishments are listed. These figures decline for all other branches of learning, with no more than seven for any one of the philosophical schools. He summarizes these findings in the following terms: †

> Amongst one hundred thousand brahmins, there †
> may be one thousand who learn the grammar of
> the Sanskrit [language]; of whom four or five hundred may read some parts of the kavya [belles lettres], and fifty some parts of the alamkara shastras [treatises on poetics]. . . . Three hundred may

study the Nyaya, but only five or six the Mimamsa, the Samkhya, the Vedanta, the Patanjala [Yoga], the Vaisesika shastras, or the Veda.[11]

It was in no small part for want of specialists in the "Patanjala" branch of Indian philosophy that Ward was unable to provide an adequate account of the *Yoga Sutra* in his early survey. A cursory reading of his translation shows it to be an adaptation at best. This was

† noted by Colebrooke, who gently chided Ward in his own 1823 study, writing that descriptions of the text "seem to have been made from an oral exposition through the medium of a different language, probably the Bengalee.... The meaning of the original is certainly not to be gathered from such translations."[12]

This state of affairs would continue well into the twentieth century: there were no pandits to be found anywhere in north India who were capable of transmitting or elucidating the teachings of the *Yoga Sutra*.

† In the middle of the nineteenth century, when James Ballantyne, the principal of the Varanasi (Benares) Government Sanskrit College, set about to produce the first English translation of the work, he noted that "no pandit in these days professes to teach the sys-

† tem."[13] Thirty years later, Rajendralal Mitra found himself at the same impasse, writing in the introduction to his 1883 *Yoga Sutra* translation that "I had hopes of reading the work with the assistance of a professional Yogi... but I could find no Pandit in Bengal who had made the Yoga the special subject of

his study."[14] Writing on the cusp of the twentieth century, Max Müller would observe in his classic *Six Systems* that among the pandits, "the Vaiseshika [philosophy] is neglected and so too is the Yoga, except in its purely practical and most degenerative form."[15]

Even before Max Müller had penned these words, however, interest in Yoga philosophy was already in the process of being revived—or perhaps reinvented— in the United States by the charismatic Indian orator Swami Vivekananda. Also prior to the close of the nineteenth century, a new explanation for the disappearance of Yoga philosophy from the Indian heartland was being proposed. Here, the story went that the "true" yogis who had not eschewed Patanjali's teachings in favor of the fanatical practices associated with Tantra, the begging bowl, or the weapons of the warrior could still be found in the seclusion of the Himalayas and beyond.

Before we leave Colebrooke and his brief, unfavorable reading of the *Yoga Sutra* behind, we need also to consider two quantifiable data sources to which the great Orientalist would not have been indifferent. Throughout his study of the six systems, Colebrooke makes reference to the commentarial traditions of each respective school, noting the "innumerable" works on Nyaya and Vedanta in particular. In fact, between 100 and 1660 CE, no fewer than 511 commentaries and subcommentaries were written on the *Nyaya* and *Vaisheshika Sutras* alone. For the same period, only a dozen commentaries and subcommentaries were

written on the *Yoga Sutra*—and of these, none, with
the exception of Bhoja's "Royal Sun," can be said to
have been composed by a proponent of Patanjali's
system. At bottom, there never was, properly speaking,
a "Yoga School" of philosophy. Between Vijnanabhikshu's two sixteenth-century works and Colebrooke's time, only seven commentaries were written
on the *Yoga Sutra*. Of these, two were Jain, and the
other five, composed by authors living and writing in
south India, generally subverted, rather than eluci-
dated, its Yoga teachings. Reading Patanjali's work
through the lens of Vedanta and Hindu devotional

† piety, they were, in effect, dismantling it. Outside of
these, only a smattering of authors even referred to the
Yoga Sutra in their writings. All of these data lead one
to conclude that by the sixteenth or seventeenth century Patanjali's Yoga system had largely become the
abandoned stepchild of Indian philosophy.

Another sort of metric further supports these conclusions. Colebrooke was a pioneer in the collection of
Indian manuscripts, which were the sole data source
for written traditions in precolonial India. Apart from
manuscripts of the *Yoga Sutra*, the oral traditions of India's yogis and pandits would have been the sole living
links to Yoga philosophy, and as we have seen, these
too had apparently disappeared by Colebrooke's time.
This may not have troubled him particularly, since as a
man of letters, he would have felt more at home with
manuscripts, and so he was. So much so that when the
India Office Library, the first British archive of Indian

manuscripts, was founded in Kolkata in 1818, Colebrooke's personal donation of some 2,749 manuscript
bundles or "codices" accounted for nearly two-thirds
of the total collection. Within that collection, 772 co- †
dices were classified under the heading of "Philosophy," and of these, 502 were from Colebrooke's personal collection. Out of those 772 codices, only
fourteen contained "Yoga" manuscripts. Eight of these
were donated by Colebrooke, but of these eight, only
five were copies of the *Yoga Sutra* or one of its commentaries: these were the sources he had used to write
his groundbreaking 1823 study. The other three titles
Colebrooke donated and listed under the "Yoga" heading were two copies of a work on Hatha Yoga and a
codex containing a number of works on Tantric Yoga.

What is most significant here are the relative numbers: the *Yoga Sutra* counts for less than 1 percent of
Colebrooke's total collection of 502 manuscripts on
the six systems. This figure may be compared with
those tabulated for manuscript codices comprising the
root texts and commentaries representative of the five
other schools:

Samkhya: ten codices (2 percent of total)
Yoga: eight codices (1.6 percent), of which five are
    Yoga Sutra and commentaries (1 percent)
Nyaya: 156 codices (32 percent)
Vaisheshika: forty-five codices (9 percent)
Mimamsa: fifty-three codices (10 percent)
Vedanta: 230 codices (46 percent)

Colebrooke's collection of *Yoga Sutra* manuscripts was minuscule in comparison to those representing the other five schools. I would argue that as much as any historical reconstruction of influences, transmissions, lineages, oral traditions, and so forth, such a quantitative assessment is, for the period we are looking at—that of the first contact between European Sanskritists and Indian philosophical works in Sanskrit—the most precise data source that one might draw upon to recreate the broad outlines of the Indian philosophical landscape. Bearing in mind the relatively short life spans of manuscripts in most south Asian climates, extant manuscript collections offer windows into which texts scribes were copying at the behest of their patrons from, in most cases, no earlier than the seventeenth century. Generally speaking, those patrons would have been royalty, members of the aristocracy, wealthy merchants, brahmin pandits, and temple and monastic institutions. These were the major sources of the manuscript collections that European Orientalists began to amass in the nineteenth century, and so they can provide us with a quantitative evaluation of the relative importance of the various schools.

Having said this, we must ask whether the same proportions would hold up if we were to look at a broader sampling (with sampling numbers being inversely proportional to margins of error). I spent a good part of the summer of 2010 engaged in the curious task of quantitative analysis, which in my case consisted of reading manuscript catalogs from India, Eu-

rope, and North America. All in all, I perused over fifty catalogs and other related sources, with special focus on India's eleven largest and most representative manuscript collections, as indicated in Philipp André †
Maas's recent extensive survey of *Yoga Sutra* manuscript traditions. This I did in order to tabulate: (1) numbers of *Yoga Sutra*–related manuscripts, including commentaries, that predated Colebrooke's 1823 study; (2) total numbers of *Yoga Sutra*–related manuscripts, both pre- and post-1823, including undated manuscripts; (3) total numbers of manuscripts on Hatha and Tantric Yoga classified under the heading of "Yoga" philosophy; and (4) total numbers of manuscripts, including commentaries, from the other philosophical schools, with a special focus on Vedanta and Nyaya-Vaisheshika manuscripts.

In the end, I found that the proportions obtaining in Colebrooke's 1818 donation to the India Office Library generally held up. Out of a total of some †
twenty thousand manuscripts listed in these catalogs on Yoga, Nyaya-Vaisheshika, and Vedanta philosophy, a mere 260 were *Yoga Sutra* manuscripts (including commentaries), with only thirty-five dating from before 1823; 513 were manuscripts on Hatha or Tantric Yoga, manuscripts of works attributed to Yajnavalkya, or of the *Yoga Vasistha*; 9,032 were Nyaya manuscripts, and 10,320 were Vedanta manuscripts. The following list breaks down these figures on a percentage basis:

Yoga Sutra manuscripts: 1.27 percent of total
   manuscripts
Yoga Sutra manuscripts: 33.6 percent of total Yoga
   philosophy manuscripts
Yoga philosophy manuscripts: 3.79 percent of total
   manuscripts
Nyaya-Vaisheshika manuscripts: 44.2 percent of
   total manuscripts
Vedanta manuscripts: 50.6 percent of total
   manuscripts

What does this quantitative analysis tell us? For every manuscript on Yoga philosophy proper (excluding Hatha and Tantric Yoga) held in major Indian manuscript libraries and archives, there exist some forty Vedanta manuscripts and nearly as many Nyaya-Vaisheshika manuscripts. Manuscripts of the *Yoga Sutra* and its commentaries account for only one-third of all manuscripts on Yoga philosophy, the other two-thirds being devoted mainly to Hatha and Tantric Yoga. But it is the figure of 1.27 percent that stands out in highest relief, because it tells us that after the late sixteenth century virtually no one was copying the *Yoga Sutra* because no one was commissioning *Yoga Sutra* manuscripts, and no one was commissioning *Yoga Sutra* manuscripts because no one was interested in reading the *Yoga Sutra*. Some have argued that instruction in the *Yoga Sutra* was based on rote memorization or chanting: this is the position of Krishnamacharya's biographers as well as of a number of critical scholars. But this is pure speculation, undercut by the nineteenth-century observations of James Ballantyne, Dayananda Saraswati, Rajendralal Mitra, Friedrich Max Müller, and others. There is no explicit record, in either the commentarial tradition itself or in the sacred or secular literatures of the past two thousand years, of adherents of the Yoga school memorizing, chanting, or claiming an oral transmission for their traditions.

Given these data, we may conclude that Colebrooke's laconic, if not hostile, treatment of the *Yoga Sutra* undoubtedly stemmed from the fact that by his time, Patanjali's system had become an empty signifier, with no traditional schoolmen to expound or defend it and no formal or informal outlets of instruction in its teachings. It had become a moribund tradition, an object of universal indifference. The *Yoga Sutra* had for all intents and purposes been lost until Colebrooke found it.

Yoga Sutra Agonistes: Hegel and the German Romantics

Now freed from its Indian moorings, the *Yoga Sutra's* westward drift next brought it to Germany, where Colebrooke's 1823 study was seized upon almost immediately by Georg W. F. Hegel, who was, in the 1820s, fully engrossed in his mammoth project of writing a world history of philosophy, and—to ensure that absolutely nothing would be left out—a philosophy of world history. Hegel's was philosophy on a grand scale. Decades before Darwin and nearly a century before depth psychology, Hegel's grand system sought to trace the evolution of the human spirit across the ages in a unique and idiosyncratic way. For Hegel, history was the stage upon which an abstract cosmic mind called the "World Spirit" evolved—from a state of unconsciousness to one of self-conscious freedom grounded in ethical responsibility—by morphing into a succession of "folk" or "national spirits" (Volksgeists) spurred by the acts of "world historical individuals" such as Napoleon for Hegel's own time.

Hegel's death in 1831 cut short many of his ambitious works in progress; however, an outline of his reading of Indian philosophy, including Yoga philosophy, may be found in his now published lecture notes †
from the 1825–26 academic year at Berlin University. Hegel made constant reference to Colebrooke in these lectures, albeit with no explicit mention of the *Yoga Sutra*. In those same lectures, Hegel made a point of mocking the writings of the brothers Friedrich and August Wilhelm von Schlegel, the founders of German Indology. Hegel's invective was particularly directed at Friedrich, the 1808 author of *Über die Sprache und Weisheit der Indier* ("On the Language and Wisdom of the Indians"), an iconic work of German Romanticism. Not known for pulling his punches, Hegel remained true to form here, dismissing Schlegel's understanding of Indian wisdom as superficial and grounded in religious rather than philosophical sources.

Hegel's most sustained discussion of the *Yoga Sutra*, viewed once again through the lens of Colebrooke's study, appeared in a set of critical essays published in †
1827. Ostensibly written as a critique of two lectures presented on the *Bhagavad Gita* in 1825 and 1826 by the remarkable Prussian polymath, Wilhelm von Humboldt, Hegel's review articles, which were substantially longer than Humboldt's lectures themselves, were in many respects a pretext for settling a number †
of scores—not only with Humboldt but also with the brothers Schlegel and, by extension, the entire Ger-

man Romantic movement. Unlike Hegel, Humboldt had a reading knowledge of Sanskrit, and his interpretation of the *Bhagavad Gita* was grounded in a linguistic analysis of its terminology. In this, he was following in the footsteps of the Schlegels. Friedrich's 1808 publication—which we see Hegel belittling in his lecture notes—had been a truly groundbreaking work of European Indology inasmuch as it was the first German-language work to use original Sanskrit-language source materials in its presentation of Indian language, literature, and history.

For the Romantics, who took their lead from the eighteenth-century enlightenment philosopher Voltaire, the golden age of humanity—the original fount of human spirituality and completeness, the lost paradise of all religions and philosophies—was to be found in ancient India. In contrast, the post-Enlightenment world in which man now found himself was a sterile, spiritually impoverished place inhabited by human "machines." Only through the wisdom of the ancient Indians, they insisted, could fallen Western man hope to find his way back to his true spiritual home. Small wonder, then, that for Schlegel, the Indian sacred literature was the "pinnacle of Romanticism," the source of all the world's languages, and "all the thoughts and poems of the human spirit."[1] Furthermore, because the peoples of Europe and Asia were part of one vast family, ancient Indian philosophy lay at the origin of *both* Eastern and Western thought. In the same way that the rediscovery of ancient Greek thought had spurred the

Italian Renaissance, Schlegel argued, the recovery of ancient Indian wisdom would give rise to a second, "Oriental" Renaissance.

Hegel had no such nostalgia for ancient Indian wisdom. Even if it could be shown that Sanskrit had been †
the mother of ancient Greek and Latin, and even if India were the "original homeland" from which the Europeans first emigrated, all of these events took place in *prehistory*, and not on the stage of history—upon which India did not appear until its colonization by the British. As for the history of philosophy, it was, by definition, European history, the ascending arc of Western thought from the pre-Socratic philosophers down to German philosophers like Hegel himself. This axiom lay at the core of Hegel's dialectic. With the awakening of consciousness to reason and moral responsibility in ancient Greece, the World Spirit, which had theretofore lain in a state of slumber, came to embrace the ancient Greek Volksgeist. Since that time it had metamorphosed via a succession of "Spirits of the Time" (Zeitgeists) through the vicissitudes of the Middle Ages and Renaissance—but always in the West, because the West alone was historical, and the †
West alone had philosophy. In such a scheme, there could be no place for a parallel or convergent Indian stream.

To be sure, India had been a cradle of religion of a particular sort, but for Hegel this was at best an "antici- †
pation of philosophy" in a culture that remained pre-historical, forever outside the sweep of history whose

culmination, the complete self-realization of the World Spirit, was none other than the Volksgeist of the modern German state. In contrast to the freedom of the self-conscious mind that defined nineteenth-century

† Germany, the Indian mind had never evolved beyond a sort of dream state in which consciousness was incapable of awakening to subjective reason. As such, the Indian mind was nonphilosophical, with what passed for Indian philosophy being nothing more than Indian religion.

† For Hegel, the epitome of the dream world of the Indian mind was, precisely, Yoga, which he termed "the innermost core of the Indian religion."[2] However, prior to Colebrooke's 1823 study, the Yoga doctrine that both the Idealist Hegel and his Romantic sparring partners were focused upon had been that of the *Bhagavad Gita*, with its classical reference to the "three yogas." It was this sacred teaching, already so highly revered by the Orientalists, that Humboldt was inter-

† preting in his lectures—but behind Humboldt's lecture stood August Wilhelm von Schlegel's Latin-language translation of the work, as well as Humboldt's own appreciation of the *Bhagavad Gita* as a full-fledged philosophical system.

Hegel's reading of Colebrooke's 1823 study greatly affected his view of the Indian Volksgeist. On the one hand, it seems to have forced him to reconsider, however briefly, the possibility of incorporating India into his vast tableau of the history of world philosophy. Since Colebrooke had clearly treated Samkhya as a philosophy, Hegel was faced with the alternatives of either building it into his world history of philosophy or refuting its status as philosophy. But Hegel had another ulterior motive: Colebrooke's study gave him an opening to take on (and take out) both Humboldt and the brothers Schlegel, and to establish himself as the German authority on Indian philosophy.

In his lectures on the *Bhagavad Gita*, Humboldt †
had defended August Wilhelm von Schlegel's translation of the term "yoga" against other Orientalist detractors, most notably the French Sanskritist Alexandre Langlois. Armed with Colebrooke's study (which he paraphrases extensively throughout his critical review), Hegel attacked Humboldt on this very point. For whereas Humboldt and Schlegel had translated †
yoga as "absorption" (Vertiefung) and "devotion of perseverance" (assiduitatis devotio) respectively, Hegel took the position that the term was simply untranslatable: "Our [German] language cannot possess a word which corresponds to such a determination because the thing cannot be found in our culture and religion."[3] Later, however, he would come around to proposing his own translation: for Hegel, yoga was "abstract devotion" (abstracte Andacht).

But the scope of Hegel's reprimands extended well beyond matters of translation, for the true aim of his review was to demonstrate that the German Romantics' vision of the *Bhagavad Gita* as philosophy was null and void, on the ground that the notion that Indian thought had a philosophical content was itself null and void. To not attack Humboldt on this point would have been tantamount to allowing that India had a philosophy, and that it was, by extension, "historical." So, indeed, much was at stake here. Commenting on a passage from the *Bhagavad Gita*'s second chapter (2.39), Hegel set up his argument:

† But Krsna adds that what he has made Arjuna to consider was according to the Samkhya doctrine; now however, he would take the standpoint of the Yoga doctrine. By this the entirely strange field of the Indian world-view is revealed. . . . Religion and philosophy, too, merge here in such a way that they seem to be at first indistinguishable. Thus right from the beginning the author [Humboldt] has called the contents of the poem . . . a complete *philosophical system*. In the history of philosophy there is in general great difficulty and confusion . . . [when one is attempting] to discover a special characteristic according to which such contents would belong to the one or the other region [i.e., religion or philosophy]. As regards Indian culture, such a distinction has now at last been made possible by means of extracts from truly philosophical works of the Indians, which Colebrooke has presented to the European public in the *Transactions of the Royal Asiatic Society*.[4]

Here it would appear that Hegel was admitting the possibility that India could have produced a philosophical system independent of religious dogma—

until he hoists Humboldt by his own petard (and with him Schlegel, since he notes that it is Schlegel's translation he is quoting):

> As Herr von Humboldt points out ... from the †
> highest Indian point of view—as this is expressed
> in *Bhagavad Gita* 5.5—this difference [between
> Samkhya philosophy and Yoga religion] disap-
> pears; both ways of thought have the one and only
> goal: *The one who understands, that the reasonable*
> (Sanc'hya Sastra) *and the religious* (Yoga Sastra) *are*
> *one and the same doctrine, is the one who verily*
> *knows.*[5]

But Hegel's coup de grâce (at least in his own mind) came not from the *Bhagavad Gita* itself, but rather from the *Yoga Sutra*. Referring to the "devout exercises †
and pious meditation" of the Yoga of Patanjali, Cole-brooke had asserted that "because religious observances are more concerned than philosophy with the topics there treated ... the ritual of the *Yóga*... would be a fitter subject of a separate treatise, rather than to be incidentally touched on while investigating the philosophical doctrines of both schools."[6] This was Hegel's opening, and he took it by arbitrarily identifying Schlegel's "devotion of perseverance" with the practices outlined in the *Yoga Sutra*'s third chapter—that is, with the techniques for attaining supernatural powers, which Colebrooke had dismissed as tanta- †
mount "to a belief of magic." At this point, the focus of Hegel's analysis drifted from Yoga philosophy as found

in the *Bhagavad Gita* and the *Yoga Sutra* to the practices of yogis, as attested by the British in India:

† What here is called *assiduitatis devotio* amounts to what Colebrooke mentions with reference to *Patanjali's Yoga-Sastra* (3rd Chap.). . . . He says that this chapter contains almost exclusively instructions for physical and mental exercises. . . . Herr von Humboldt refers to this passage and concludes . . . that it seems that the gazing meditation of the Yogi would also have been fixed on other things than the Godhead. . . . The Indian isolation of the soul into emptiness is rather a stupefaction which perhaps does not at all deserve the name mysticism and which cannot lead to the discovery of true insights, because it is void of any contents. . . . Now what the Yogi first of all achieves through the devotion of perseverance is the miraculous ability of an *unlimited power*. . . . Yogis and magicians are . . . for the Indian *masses* synonymous terms. One could misunderstand this in the sense that the belief in such a power could only be found among common people. Colebrooke, however, remarks in that passage that the Yoga doctrine of Patanjali, as well as the Sanc'hya doctrine maintain that man can achieve in this life such a transcendent power.[7]

† Hegel concludes his review with a wholesale rejection of the Indian worldview as superficial, derivative, and utterly alien to the European mind. Yet it would ap-

pear that Colebrooke's study had planted some seeds of doubt in Hegel's mind with respect to Indian philosophy, which even his quarrels with the brothers Schlegel could not supplant. So we see him, in the two years prior to his death in 1831, returning to a consideration of the philosophical content of both Samkhya and the *Yoga Sutra*. Colebrooke's influence had already † appeared in Hegel's 1827 review of Humboldt's lectures, for in them he had cast Yoga as the "midpoint between Indian religion and philosophy." Now, in his † 1829–30 lectures on the history of philosophy, he returned to the *Yoga Sutra*, singling out its final chapter, on "abstraction or spiritual isolation" (samadhi), as "philosophy proper." In spite of this, he never took the † next step of incorporating Indian philosophy into his grand scheme of the history of philosophy. It may be that death overtook him before he could do so. However, it is more likely that he never would have made such a move because Eastern philosophy could never have passed his litmus test for philosophy, which was the passage from abstraction to conceptualization. Therefore, just as history, which had begun in Asia, was "ahistorical history," so too Eastern philosophy was "nonphilosophical philosophy."

For all his pontificating, bluster, and Eurocentrism, Hegel did prove capable, in the end, of at least lending serious consideration to Indian philosophy. This is no small thing. As Robert Bernasconi, from whose fine essay on this chapter in Hegel's intellectual biography I have drawn extensively here, concludes,

†   after reading the *Yoga-Sutras*, Hegel granted that there had been an Indian philosophy and that we could learn from it. . . . Hegel was more open to the possibility of Indian philosophy, and more ready to look at the latest research about it, than many of us Western philosophers are even today. An examination of the way philosophy is taught in most departments in North America and Europe would confirm that the institutions of philosophy are still for the most part on the wrong side of even Hegel on this issue, and that should be enough to set the alarm bells ringing.[8]

If Hegel is deserving of some praise for his Teutonic blessing of Indian philosophy, and the *Yoga Sutra* specifically, as worthy of admission onto the stage of the history of "true" philosophy, he must nonetheless be faulted on another account. Here I am speaking of the ease with which he established himself as an expert on Yoga philosophy on the basis of his reading of Colebrooke's short 1823 study. With no reading ability in Sanskrit and no access to the primary source material he was interpreting, he nonetheless felt himself authorized to pontificate on the (in)validity of Yoga philosophy as philosophy. As we will see, he was but the first in a long line of dilettantes, both Western and Indian, who have interpreted the *Yoga Sutra* on the basis of little or no understanding as means to furthering their own agendas.

Rajendralal Mitra

INDIA'S FORGOTTEN PIONEER OF
YOGA SUTRA SCHOLARSHIP

CHAPTER 5

It was not until twenty-nine years after Colebrooke's
groundbreaking study that James Ballantyne brought
out the earliest partial English translation of the *Yoga
Sutra*, in 1852. Ballantyne's unfinished translation of
the *Yoga Sutra* would not be completed until 1871,
when a pandit named Govinda Shastri Deva translated its final two chapters—"in a disjointed way" ac-   †
cording to Rajendralal Mitra—in successive issues of a   †
Varanasi review titled "The Pandit." However, the
complete Ballantyne–Shastri Deva translation did not
appear in a single bound volume until two years after
the publication of Mitra's own 1883 translation. Like
the Ballantyne–Shastri Deva collaboration, Mitra's
translation of the *Yoga Sutra* included Bhoja's commentary. All resemblance between the two ends here,
however, as Mitra's work far outshines not only that of
Ballantyne–Shastri Deva but also the majority of
translations that have been attempted since. Largely
overlooked in both academic and popular circles, Mi-

tra's is an important work of erudition and an essential chapter in the history of critical Yoga scholarship. His extensive hundred-page preface and incisive commentary were an exponential advance over Colebrooke's brief overview of 1823, making his the first scholarly volume entirely dedicated to an excavation of the *Yoga Sutra*. Here one finds, among many other things, the

† earliest comprehensive investigation into the "historical" Patanjali and the relationship between the author of the *Yoga Sutra* and the other Patanjalis of the Indian history of ideas. In spite of its importance, Mitra's contribution is conspicuously absent from nearly every historical survey, which leap from Colebrooke's study to lesser overviews by Richard Garbe (1896) and Max Müller (1899). Published in the prestigious "Bibliotheca Indica" series, it has long been out of print, with only a handful of copies extant, which perhaps accounts for its neglect.

In the summer of 2011, I was able to procure a microfilm copy of Mitra's work through the University of California's interlibrary loan system. What I read came as a revelation of sorts. As we saw in chapter 2, the philosophical system of the *Yoga Sutra*—that is, the bulk of the text, leaving aside its instructions on the eight-part practice—is not simple. No doubt for this reason a small army of critical scholars, yoga gurus, and yoga enthusiasts of every stripe has for the past century been churning out volumes of printed page attempting to explicate the subtleties of that system. In doing so, nearly all have adhered to the format of commentarial convention, slavishly following the order of the sutras as they are found in the original text. However, as Ram Shankar Bhattacharya (who coedited the massive and authoritative "encyclopedia" of Yoga together with Gerald James Larson) has observed, Patanjali's original ordering cannot but confuse the modern mind: "the † arrangement is not at all helpful to persons of modern times in understanding the doctrines of yoga in an eas-ier way."[1] S. Radhakrishnan is less charitable: for him † Patanjali's system is fundamentally incoherent. In other words, by following the order of the sutras, one loses the forest for the trees. Over the past century, sev-eral metaphorical forests have been lost in this way. Be-cause much of this book is devoted to the ways in which people have interpreted Patanjali's system, I find it useful to reproduce Mitra's summary of its fun-damental axioms, which he presents with a succinct-ness and clarity I have not found elsewhere.

What follows is taken nearly verbatim from Mitra. I † have, however, edited some of his quaint nineteenth-century expressions, replacing them with their modern synonyms, which are indicated in square brackets. A term that frequently appears in Mitra's summary is "noumenon," a term he explicitly borrows from Kan-tian philosophy, to refer to a "thing-in-itself," that is, an object directly apprehended by the mind or intel-lect, and not by the senses (in which case it is called a "phenomenon"). This is Mitra's translation of the San-skrit word *tattva*, which I translated in chapter 2 as "entity," "principle," or "substrate." Mitra also translates

Purusha as "soul" rather than "Person" or "Spirit," and I have retained his usage here. Mitra divides his exposition into seventeen sequenced points. One only wishes that Patanjali had presented his system in the same way, since it would have made the *Yoga Sutra* far more accessible:

1st.   That there is a Supreme Godhead (Ishvara) who is purely spiritual, or all soul, perfectly free from afflictions, works, deserts, and desires. His symbol is Om, and He rewards those who are ardently devoted to Him by facilitating their attainment of liberation; but He does not directly grant it. Nor is He the father, creator, or protector of the universe, with which He is absolutely unconnected.

2nd.   That there are countless individual souls (Purushas) that animate living beings and are eternal. They are pure and immutable, but by their association with the universe they become indirectly the experiencers of joys and sorrows and assume innumerable embodied forms in course of ever recurring [reincarnation].

3rd.   That the universe is uncreate[d] and eternal. It undergoes phenomenal changes, but, as a noumenon, it is always the same. In its noumenal state it is called *Prakriti* or nature; it is always associated with the three qualities or active forces (gunas).... Matter as an integral part of the universe is, likewise, eternal, though subject to modifications like the world. Strictly speaking, the modifications of matter produce the phenomenal world, which is composed of it.

4th. That next to the soul there is a noumenon called *citta*, or the thinking principle, or mind in its most comprehensive sense. It is subject to the three qualities aforesaid and undergoes various modifications according to the prevalence of one or other of these qualities. It is essentially unconscious or unintelligent, but it becomes conscious or intelligent by the reflection of, or association with, soul, which abides close by it. It also receives through the organs of sense shadows of external objects, and thereupon modifies itself into the shapes of those objects. The consciousness reflected on it makes it think that it is the experiencer of all worldly joys and sorrows. In reality, however, it is merely the spectacle of which the soul is by proxy (its shadow) the spectator.

5th. That the functions of the thinking principle are five-fold, including right notion, misconception, fancy, sleep, and memory, and that these functions are produced by the prevalence of one or other of the three qualities.

6th. That like the universe, all sensible objects have their eternal archetypes or noumena, which undergo phenomenal changes, but are never absolutely destroyed. When one object changes into another, it is merely a modification of its form, and the form assumed, when destroyed, passes on to some other form, but it ultimately reverts to its noumenal or primary state.

7th. That phenomena, as results of modifications of noumena, are real and not phantasmal.

8th. That [sense-objects] are not the direct causes of sensations, nor sensations the causes of [sense-objects]; but that the thinking principle receives impressions of [sense-objects] under the influence of one or other of the three qualities, and the result is regulated by that influence. The influence extends both to sensations and to [sense-objects].

9th. That the thinking principle being changeable, constancy of knowledge is due to the immutability of the soul, and that no perception can take place until the thinking principle is made conscious by the soul.

10th. That impressions produced on the thinking principle leave on it certain [residues] ... which are the causes of intuitions, desires, new births, and further experience.

11th. That desires are the origin of pain in the world.

12th. That the universe being eternal, desires are likewise eternal, and it is needless therefore to inquire when [residues] first arose to create desires.

13th. That mundane existence is thus associated with pain, and it is the duty of everyone to rise above that pain.

14th. That the pain may be finally overcome or removed only by withdrawing the thinking principle from its natural functions.

15th. That the withdrawal in question can be effected by constant and sedulous observance of certain prescribed restraints, obligations, and steadfast meditation.

16th. That in the course of the exercises above referred to, the adept attains extraordinary occult powers.

17th. That when that withdrawal is complete and absolute, the soul is completely isolated from the world, and that when that isolation is attained, it is liberated from all liability to future transmigration. And this is the isolation, liberation, emancipation, or final beatitude, which should be the great object and aim of human existence.[2]

Mitra's reading of the *Yoga Sutra* is colored throughout by Bhoja's commentary, of which he was highly appreciative. His opinion of Vyasa, whom Bhoja "treated with withering sarcasm," is quite the opposite, as evidenced in his evaluation of the "Commentary" as "the production of a third class writer."[3] I have already noted Mitra's opinion of India's yogis, and his distinction between their delusional vagaries and Yoga philosophy itself. Elsewhere, Mitra expands on the division of labor among scholars, ascetics (whom he distinguishes from yogis), and pandits:

† The subject is dry—exceedingly so—and the enigmatical form in which it is presented in the textbooks is not conducive to any interest being created in its favour. Generally speaking Indian scholars do not study it, and the few ascetics and hermits who do seldom associate with the world. Pandits, when called upon to explain, frequently, if not invariably, mix up the tenets of Patanjali's Yoga with those of the Tantras, the Puranas . . . and the Bhagavad Gita—works which have very dissimilar and discordant tenets to inculcate.[4]

In a Hindu India that was firmly entrenched in (Neo-) Vedanta philosophy, interest in the *Yoga Sutra* did not begin to awaken in intellectual circles until Mitra's pioneering translation. As for the ascetics and hermits evoked here, we see Mitra subscribing to a perennial Indian tradition concerning the Himalayas as a kind of Shangri-la, the pristine haunt of authentic sages in whose entranced minds all of India's ancient wisdom had survived intact. As I mentioned earlier, Mitra had unsuccessfully attempted to find a "professional yogi"

† or pandit to guide him in his translation project—although he does speak of a person in Varanasi who would have apprenticed him, had he, Mitra, been ready to live in his hut and follow in his footsteps to

† the end of his days. Like Colebrooke before him, Mitra relied on his own knowledge of Sanskrit for his translation, but he also acknowledges the aid of two Nyaya

and Samkhya specialists from the Kolkata Sanskrit College, as well as his dependence on Colebrooke's translation of a treatise on Samkhya for his own translations of technical terms.

Most interesting is Mitra's account of India's pandits. As was noted with respect to Colebrooke's "rediscovery" of the *Yoga Sutra*, Yoga philosophy had been effectively dropped from the traditional north Indian brahmanic curriculum by no later than the sixteenth century. With no living link to Patanjali's text and its commentarial tradition, the pandits, when asked, would do what pandits have always done: string together what they knew about Yoga—mainly from the Puranas and Smriti literature, but also from Tantric and Hatha Yoga traditions—and identify that amalgam with the teachings of the *Yoga Sutra*. In any case, as the custodians of Hindu tradition, they would have had no reason to familiarize themselves with a work from which God as they knew it was absent. This is very important, because it continues to be the case with nearly every modern yoga guru, including the illustrious Vivekananda, Krishnamacharya, and Yogi Bikram. The so-called *Yoga Sutra* the gurus have been teaching their Western followers for over a century has been the eight-part practice of the Puranas and various other scraps of yoga lore known to the pandits. It has precious little in common with the philosophical *Yoga Sutra* of Patanjali and his classical commentators. To be sure, every classical commentator beginning with Vyasa did quote from the Puranas, *Bhagavad Gita*, and other works; however, they referred to them to illustrate points of Yoga philosophy rather than to substitute them for a lack of knowledge of the same.

Mitra also took a hardheaded approach toward Western philosophers and Indologists whom he saw as playing fast and loose with the content and coherence
† of the Yoga system. One of these was the German Indologist Albrecht Weber, who, like so many others, had read the *Yoga Sutra* through the lens of Advaita Vedanta. Weber, who identified *kaivalyam*—the final isolation of Spirit from Nature—with "absorption into the supreme Godhead," was taken to task by Mitra, who suggested that Weber had never read the *Yoga Sutra* but had rather based his interpretation on the *Bhagavad Gita* and Puranic and Tantric modifications of Yoga philosophy. Ditto the French philosopher Victor Cousin, who had defined *kaivalyam* as "absolute nihilism, the final fruit of skepticism."[5] Here, Mitra responded by reminding his reader that since Yoga philosophy posits the continuing existence— rather than the annihilation—of the soul after death, the claim of nihilism was unfounded.

Ever attentive to presenting the philosophy of the
† *Yoga Sutra* as philosophy, Mitra noted that those aspects of Patanjali's system that appeared unworthy of philosophical inquiry had their parallels in Western ways of thought. This included the positing of universal categories or noumena, which he compared to those of both the ancient Greek and nineteenth-century Continental philosophers. Noting that "the

two most repellent dogmas of the system are its faith in metempsychosis [i.e., transmigration of the soul] and occult powers," he allowed that "carefully considered, they do not seem to be so absurd as one would at first glance suppose."[6] Concerning transmigration, Mitra, who knew his Classics, pointed to its presence in Plato's writings. Quoting an English clergyman, he also noted that the Hindu doctrine of karma and rebirth was a more satisfying explanation for theodicy, the problem of evil, than the Christian doctrine of predestination. With respect to the occult powers that are the subject of the *Yoga Sutra*'s third chapter, he compared them to "mesmeric and other conditions of the body [that] are now objects of scientific research."[7] In fact, the Magnetic System—also known as Mesmerism in recognition of its founder, the German physician Franz Anton Mesmer—was all the rage during the final decades of the nineteenth century, at which time many considered it to be hard science, as opposed to mere scientism. This was the position taken by a certain Madame Helena Petrovna Blavatsky, whose 1877 occult blockbuster, *Isis Unveiled*, drew heavily upon the theory of animal magnetism and all that went with it.

The Yoga of the Magnetosphere
THE *YOGA SUTRA* AND THE THEOSOPHICAL SOCIETY

CHAPTER 6

In 1875 the Russian émigré Madame Blavatsky founded the Theosophical Society in New York City together with fellow occultists William Quan Judge and Colonel Henry Steel Olcott. Accomplished spirit mediums themselves, Blavatsky and Olcott were deeply committed to reforming the spiritualist movement that had been sweeping the Anglo-American world since 1848, when the Fox sisters, a pair of teenage girls from the Rochester area of upstate New York, had begun to hear rapping sounds made by spirits of the dead coming up through the floorboards of their house. Apart from her own exotic background, charisma, and sophistication, what set Blavatsky apart from the American spiritualists were the outstanding personal contacts she had with an international cast of spirits. Towering over all of these polyglot clackers of the ether was an elite group she claimed to have run into in the magnetosphere above Tibet, called the "Himalayan Masters"—one of whom, as she later claimed, had directly dictated

Isis Unveiled to her. As it turns out, Blavatsky's Masters had been reading many of the same books as she: within a year of its publication, William Emmette Coleman, a critical scholar and member of the American Oriental Society and Pali Text Society, denounced Blavatsky for some two thousand instances of plagiarism he had found in her book. The negative fallout from these and other scandals prompted Blavatsky and Olcott to decamp for India in 1878, leaving the leadership of the stateside organization to Abner Doubleday, the legendary inventor of American baseball. †

Once on Indian soil, Blavatsky revealed that the "Masters" she had been channeling were in fact "Mahatmas," a Sanskrit term meaning "Great Souls," and that the most important among these—Koot Hoomi and Master Morya—were Indian spirits. Blavatsky's odyssey halfway around the world had brought her nearly within shouting distance of her closest sources from the other side. In 1882, after the society had moved into its new headquarters in Adyar on the outskirts of Chennai, the capital of what would become the southern state of Tamil Nadu, chatter from the Mahatmas increased in both quality and quantity, as hundreds of handwritten letters began to materialize in the shrine room adjacent to Blavatsky's private living quarters. These, too, alas, turned out to be fabrications, written for the most part in Blavatsky's own hand and delivered through hidden wall panels. In 1885, the British Society for Psychical Research de- †

clared Blavatsky a patent fraud, devoting 174 pages of its *Proceedings* to arguing its case against her. Under this new cloud of scandal, Blavatsky left India for Europe that same year, but nonetheless soldiered on, publishing *The Secret Doctrine* in 1885.

In spite of its founders' misadventures, the Theosophical Society may be credited with having projected yoga onto the magnetosphere of the late nineteenth-century Indian and Western consciousness, since it was through its efforts—far more than those of Colebrooke, Hegel, or Mitra—that a distinction between Yoga and the highly problematic lifestyles of the Indian yogis first began to emerge. In her not uncharacteristic hyperbolic way, Madame Blavatsky took full credit for these developments, asserting in 1881 that "neither modern Europe nor America had so much as heard [of yoga] until the Theosophists began to speak and write."[1] There was no small amount of truth to her claim. As it happens, the society's Mumbai publishing house was responsible for bringing out two of the earliest translations of the *Yoga Sutra*, both of which were composed by Indian members of the society: Tookaram Tatya's edition of the Ballantyne–Shastri Deva collaboration in 1885, and a translation by M. N. Dvivedi in 1890. Far more influential in Western occult circles was an entirely superficial "interpretation" of the *Yoga Sutra* that Judge authored in 1888. Yet another translation, also published by the society, would appear in 1907: this was the work of Ganganath

Jha, a highly accomplished Sanskrit scholar and pur-
ported mentor of Krishnamacharya, about whom
more in chapter 12.

Like everything else about her worldview, Blavatsky's position on yoga was highly convoluted. On †
the one hand, she glorified what she called "Raja Yoga"
over and against the physical practices of Hatha Yoga,
which she considered to be inferior. Yet concerning
the yogis themselves, she took a contrarian position
with respect to the general Western censure of them,
showing great respect for their miracles and remarkable physical and psychological abilities. This might †
explain some of the yogi-type conjuring tricks that
her critics accused her of performing herself, as well as †
a number of infamous "demonstrations" of yogic powers by society-approved disciples of the great Mahatmas, which at times degenerated into full-blown fias-
cos with blood on the floor. Due perhaps to Blavatsky's disdain for Hatha Yoga, the society waited until
after her demise before it began publishing English-
language translations of important late Hatha Yoga
texts, including the *Shiva Samhita* ("Shiva's Collection," 1893), the *Hathayoga Pradipika* ("Little Lamp of
Hatha Yoga," 1893), and *Gheranda Samhita* ("Gheranda's Collection," 1895).

The Theosophists' motives for rehabilitating Indian
Yoga (as they understood it) were both philosophical
and political. Even after its embrace of Eastern spirituality, the society remained committed to the Anglo-
American spiritualism that had been responsible for

launching the movement in the first place. Already in *Isis Unveiled*, Blavatsky had asserted that all that existed in the universe was bathed in "ether," an "astral

† light" or "magnetic fluid." This was her channel of communication with the Masters and Mahatmas, as well as the energizing principle of all of matter or nature, which, when controlled, could heal, harmonize,

† and transform human life. Here, her most obvious inspiration was Mesmer's Magnetic System, according to which an invisible fluid connected all parts of the universe, both spiritual and material: this is the fluid one sees in "ectoplasmic photographs" linking mediums

† and the spirits they are channeling during séances. As she became more familiar with Indian terminology, Blavatsky expanded her metaphysical vocabulary to include both "atman" (which she identified as the "universal spirit") and "prana" ("the active power producing all vital phenomena") in her 1885 *Secret Doc-*

† *trine*. A few years later, the Theosophist Shrinivasa Iyangar would translate prana as "the magnetic current or breath" in his 1893 edition and translation of the "Little Lamp."

At a relatively early date, Blavatsky and other Theosophists had seized upon Yoga as a prime example of an ancient and authentically Indian science, and so they promoted its teachings through lectures, demonstrations, and the publication of foundational texts.

† Under the direction of Annie Besant, who succeeded Blavatsky in India in 1893, the society's activities became increasingly directed against the British colonial

and missionary presence in India. As heirs to the Orientalist Renaissance, Romanticism, and spiritualism, the Theosophists were predisposed to anticolonialism and anticlericalism because they believed that India was the original and authentic home of all of human spirituality. The wisdom of ancient Indians also provided a solid scientific foundation for Theosophical spirituality—the séances, ectoplasmic apparitions, and so on. On the first count, many of the Theosophists' positions meshed with those of the Indian leaders of the rising Indian nationalist movement. In 1916 Besant cofounded Banaras Hindu University with the expressed purpose of countering the effects of the many Christian institutions of higher education the British had established. She became increasingly active in Indian nationalist politics and was interned by the British in 1917 for her involvement in the movement. A decade earlier, in a series of lectures titled "An Introduction to Yoga," Besant strongly argued for the scientific foundations of Yoga—which she viewed, following Swami Vivekananda, as necessary to reaching the final stage of human evolution, from man to superman—but showed reserve with respect to the applicability of the *Yoga Sutra* to modern yoga practice:

> The other part of the Yoga literature is a small book   †
> called the sutras of Patanjali. That is available, but I
> am afraid that few are able to make much of it by
> themselves. In the first place, to elucidate the
> Sutras, which are simply headings, there is a great

deal of commentary in Sanskrit, only partially translated. And even the commentaries have this peculiarity, that all the most difficult words are merely repeated, not explained, so that the student is not much enlightened.[2]

Others were less circumspect. In 1927, the English Theosophist Alice Bailey published a book titled *The Light of the Soul: Its Science and Effect*. A "paraphrase" of the *Yoga Sutra*, her book drew on extant translations of and commentaries on Patanjali's work, even if, as she asserted, the sutras had been telepathically dictated to her by a "Tibetan Brother" of the "Trans-Himalayan School."[3] Bailey identified the *Yoga Sutra* with "Raja Yoga," which would, as she prophesied, "find its greatest demonstration in the West" due to the fact that the "fifth root race" of the "fifth Aryan sub-race" would reach its fullest flower among the Anglo-Saxons of Europe and the American southwest, possibly in the year 2026. This evolutionist and fundamentally racist theory was—like many of the improbable links Bailey found between Raja Yoga, Christianity, Theosophy, and other spiritualist systems—Blavatskyan in everything but name.

A far more influential publication with respect to the Western reception of Yoga philosophy was the Theosophist Ernest Wood's 1932 *Raja Yoga: The Occult Training of the Hindus*, which was later republished under the title *The Seven Schools of Yoga: An Introduction*. In it, Wood identified the first of these seven

schools as the "Raja Yoga of Patanjali." This was followed by the "Karma and Buddhi Yogas of Shri Krishna," and the "Jnana Yoga of Shri Shankaracharya." However, as Wood affirmed, all three of these fell under the heading "Raja Yoga," while the other four—Hatha, Laya, Bhakti, and Mantra Yoga—were all forms of Hatha Yoga. Wood's explanation of the term   †
"Raja" was etymological: "It is *raja* or kingly yoga, because in each case the aspirant aims at becoming completely master of himself and of his own life."[4] In 1959 Wood published a widely read Penguin paperback under the simple title of *Yoga*, in which he identified the *Yoga Sutra* as a "Raja Yoga manual." Here, Wood was undoubtedly taking his cue from Swami Vivekananda, who had burst on the late nineteenth-century scene as the greatest *Yoga Sutra* missionary of all time and who simply equated Patanjali's system with Raja Yoga. As we will see, Vivekananda's interpretation would set the mold, for better or for worse, for much of the twentieth century.

Although Wood and Bailey were Theosophists, it is important to note that Madame Blavatsky had herself had a more nuanced understanding of Raja Yoga than they. That is, even as she considered Raja Yoga to be the antitype of Hatha Yoga, she at no time identified it with the teachings of the *Yoga Sutra*. Blavatsky had de-   †
lineated her position on Hatha and Raja Yoga in a series of short articles written in the 1880 and 1881 issues of *The Theosophist*. Although she did mention Patanjali once in these studies, she never explicitly linked his sys-

tem to Raja Yoga. Rather, she singled out "Shankara's Dandi[n]s of Northern India, especially those who are settled in Rajputana," as the sole persons capable of giving "some correct notions about the Raja-Yoga."[5] The Dandins ("Staff Bearers") are a group of ten orders of high-caste Shaiva ascetics whose monastic institutions, in both north and south India, have ranked among the most powerful in the country for several centuries. While there is no record of any association between these monastic institutions and the propagation of the *Yoga Sutra* in Rajputana, in India's northwest, there was a Yoga revival in these milieus in Tamil Nadu, in south India, in the seventeenth and eighteenth centuries. In fact, most of the extant post-sixteenth-century commentaries on the *Yoga Sutra* were written by one or another member of a single intellectual lineage, one of whose founding gurus, Bhavaganesha Dikshita, was a disciple of Vijnanabhikshu himself. These were the Dikshitas, an illustrious line of scholars linked to royal courts, Dandin monasteries, and Shaiva temples in Tamil Nadu throughout this period. Like Vijnanabhikshu, the Dikshitas' reading of the *Yoga Sutra* featured an eclectic blend of Yoga and Vedanta philosophy. The same period also saw the compilation of a number of late Yoga Upanishads, as well as a commentary on the same, by a Shaiva preceptor from the same region. Like the Dikshitas' commentaries, these works also present Yoga as a subsidiary form of either Nondualist or Qualified Nondualist Vedanta philosophy. Another south Indian brahmin, the seventeenth-century

Narayana Tirtha, was the first commentator to inte- †
grate Hatha Yoga into a commentary on the *Yoga Sutra*,
and to list Raja Yoga as the highest of fifteen different
Yoga systems.

For a time, one of Blavatsky's closest associates was
himself a Dandin ascetic. This was Dayananda Saras- †
wati, the legendary founder of the reform movement
known as the Arya Samaj, or "Society of Nobles," with
which the Theosophical Society had briefly merged to
form the "Theosophical Society of the Arya Samaj"
between 1878 and 1882. After taking initiation from a
Staff Bearer in 1848, Saraswati had embarked on a
nine-year search for authentic practitioners of Yoga.
Although he never found them "even in a suicidal
hunt," his autobiography does mention a number of
itinerant Staff Bearers who instructed him in the "Science of Yoga" at various hermitages and monasteries
scattered across the mountainous regions of the subcontinent, including in the south. These may have
been the last remnants of a south Indian "*Yoga Sutra*
revival" that had flourished in these Shaiva milieus in
earlier centuries. While Saraswati mentions the writings of Patanjali in his memoirs, he nowhere identifies
either the *Yoga Sutra* or the teachings of the yogis he
met as Raja Yoga.

While we cannot know for certain whether Blavatsky's avoidance of identifying the *Yoga Sutra* with
Raja Yoga arose from things Saraswati had told her,
her reason for broaching the subject at all is announced
in the title of her 1880–81 *Theosophist* articles: "Com-

ment on *A Treatise on the Yoga Philosophy*." Hers is in fact the review of a book that had been written some thirty years earlier by an Indian surgeon named N. C. Paul. Paul's choice of a title for his book (of which the third edition was published by the Theosophical Society in 1888) was unusual inasmuch as it contained no discussion whatsoever of Yoga philosophy. Rather, what Paul focused on nearly exclusively were the salutary qualities of Hatha Yoga techniques, as well as the documented practices of illustrious yogis, all viewed from a medical perspective.

In his *Treatise*, Paul divided yoga into two types. The first of these he termed Raja Yoga—which he identified with the eight-part practice—and the second Hatha Yoga. However, his description of Raja Yoga concentrated nearly exclusively on breath control techniques as discussed in Hatha Yoga and Tantric Yoga traditions, but not found anywhere in the *Yoga Sutra* itself. Paul's confusion concerning the relationship (if any) between Raja Yoga and the contents of the *Yoga Sutra* has been widely shared. In fact, in the annals of the history of yoga, few terms have been as nebulous (and abused) as "Raja Yoga." Since the eleventh century, the period that saw the appearance of the earliest Hatha Yoga texts, the semantic field of Hatha Yoga has remained relatively stable, denoting breath control, inner locks and seals, practices of bodily purification—and, particularly in later works, postures. Also figuring in Hatha Yoga works are discussions of the networks of energy centers (chakras) and breath channels (nadis) of the yogic body: for the most part, these are borrowed from earlier works on Tantric Yoga.

What most early writings have in common in their accounts of these two types of yoga is their casting of Raja as the antitype of Hatha. None of these, however, identifies Raja Yoga with the system of the *Yoga Sutra*; rather, they link it to teachings from the Tantras and Nondualist Vedanta philosophy. A case in point, †
which anticipated Paul's transposition of the meanings of Hatha and Raja Yoga, was the 1363 *Sharngadhara Paddhati* ("Sharngadhara's Step-by-Step Guide"). For Sharngadhara, Raja Yoga denoted the practices of raising the kundalini, the female "serpent energy," through the chakras, by means of which the practitioner's body would become flooded with nectar, transforming him into a Siddha, a "Perfected Being." As for Hatha Yoga, it was of two sorts, of which the second was none other than the eight-part practice. However, as had been the case with the Puranas, the early Hatha Yoga canon did not acknowledge Patanjali as the source of its practice: the thirteenth-century *Dattatreyayogashastra* ("Datta- †
treya's Teaching on Yoga"), the first text to truly expound on Hatha Yoga and call it as such, teaches that the techniques of *hatha* are supplementary to the eight-part practice as taught by Yajnavalkya and others—but not by Patanjali.

The earliest work to contrast these two forms of yoga was the eleventh- to twelfth-century *Amanaska* †
Yoga ("Non-Mental Yoga"), which maintained that

Hatha Yoga was simply a preliminary to Raja Yoga, so-

† called because "it is the king of all Yogas."[6] Vidyaranya's fourteenth-century commentary on the *Aparoksanu-bhuti* ("Unrivaled Bull of Knowledge"), one of a legion of works spuriously attributed to Shankara, identified Raja Yoga as the "Yoga of Vedanta," with no relationship whatsoever to Patanjali's system. As for Hatha Yoga, for Vidyaranya this was Patanjali's Yoga system: in other words, Raja Yoga was the Yoga *not* found in the *Yoga Sutra*. It would not be until the fifteenth century, with Svatmaraman's "Little Lamp," a late but highly influential work, that the Hatha-Raja distinction became codified in ways similar to modern-day usages, with Hatha referring to physical techniques

† and Raja to meditative practice. The "Little Lamp" identified Raja Yoga with samadhi, the final goal of the eight-part practice, but, like the Puranas and "Yajnavalkya's Yoga," equated it with the union or identity of the individual and universal Soul. In fact, the pattern that emerges out of some eight hundred years of classifying these yoga systems is the more or less constant equation of the eight-part practice with *Hatha* Yoga, and a general disregard of the other 164 verses of the *Yoga Sutra*. All of this would change, however, in the final years of the nineteenth century.

Swami Vivekananda and the Mainstreaming of the *Yoga Sutra*

In Kolkata and greater Bengal, the administrative and intellectual center of the British Raj, Vedanta-inspired spirituality came to be increasingly embraced by India's urban elites as a compelling Hindu response to the missionary colonialism of British Christendom. Here, the founders of the leading Indian reform movement known as the Brahmo Samaj fused Nondualist Vedanta with the various currents of Western humanism, spiritualism, esotericism, and social reform that had been introduced there by Unitarian churchmen in the early nineteenth century. These leaders—Rammohun Roy (1774–1833), Debendranath Tagore (1817–1905), and Keshub Chunder Sen (1838–1884)—drew upon Indian spirituality and Western esotericism to craft a hybrid form of Vedanta, known as Neo-Vedanta, whose modern-day adherents include several New Age movements and Hindu nationalist organizations as well as nearly every twentieth and twenty-first century Indian and Western yoga guru.

As its name indicates, the philosophical foundation for Neo-Vedanta was Vedanta, which had long since become the predominant philosophical school of Hindu India. As was noted in chapter 2, the process of Vedanta-izing the *Yoga Sutra*, already well underway in the Puranas, had by the sixteenth century culminated in the nearly total eclipse of Dualist Samkhya–Yoga as a viable philosophical system. So it was that by the nineteenth century, a consensus had emerged among Indian pandits and intellectuals that the doctrines of all six schools were but complementary perspectives on a unified Indian system of knowledge, the highest expression of which was Vedanta. This perspective was given eloquent expression by Max Müller, who in his 1899 *Six Systems of Indian Philosophy* identified Vedanta as India's perennial philosophy:

† The longer I have studied the various systems, the more have I become impressed with the truth of the view taken by Vijnana-Bhikshu and others that there is behind the variety of the six systems a common fund of what may be called national or popular philosophy . . . from which each thinker was allowed to draw for his own purposes. A friend of mine, a native of India, whom I consulted about the various degrees of popularity enjoyed at the present day by different systems of philosophy in his own country, informs me that the only system that can now be said to be living in India is the Vedanta with its branches. . . . The Vedanta, being

mixed with religion, he writes, has become a living faith, and numerous Pandits can be found to-day ... who have learnt at least the principal works by heart and can expound them.[1]

Published in the same year as Max Müller's survey, Monier-Williams's *Sanskrit-English Dictionary* also bore witness to this shift, characterizing the Yoga system in a Vedanta mode as "the means by which the human spirit may attain complete union with Isvara or the Supreme Spirit."[2]

Carrying forward the legacy of the Romantics, an essential feature of Neo-Vedanta is its doctrine of Indian exceptionalism in matters historical, spiritual, and scientific. The two are intimately entwined, since, as the proponents of Neo-Vedanta have argued, all that is new in Western science was already fully mastered by enlightened Indian sages several millennia ago and written into the sacred teachings of the Veda. As for spirituality, while it is universal to all world religions, it is nowhere as pure and lofty as in Indian Vedanta, and nowhere as corrupted as in Western Christianity. The West, therefore, has much to learn from India, on both counts. Here the nineteenth-century Brahmo Samajis were working from the same page as the Theosophists and their spiritualist brethren, inasmuch as both groups viewed spiritualism as an experimental and verifiable scientific enterprise. Also common to both groups was the notion that true religious authority was rooted in rational faith and the direct revelation that arises through individual experience, intuition, and introspection. The divine was within, here and now, rather than cocooned in a distant past whose traditions were only recoverable through institutionalized religion. Those institutions, now ossified and corrupted through priest-craft, were impediments rather than conduits to any true experience of the divine.

For all of these reasons, this new universal, rational religion, this return to the luminous life-world of the forest-dwelling sages who first received and revealed the Vedas and Upanishads, required new institutions—or, rather, a reform of existing institutions, which could only be realized through a return to the

† pristine lifestyles of yore. To this end, Keshub Chunder Sen began to experiment with spiritually based communal lifestyles, conceived as modern recreations of the ashrams of the ancient sages. Sen's early career in the Brahmo Samaj leadership had unfolded under the sign of social activism: lectures, meetings, publishing projects, and the founding of educational institutions.

† An 1875 meeting with the ecstatic hermit Ramakrishna, a living icon of Bengali spirituality, changed all that, with Sen turning increasingly to meditation and hearkening to the voice of God within. In this he was also influenced by the American Transcendentalists, whose writings were another important source of inspiration.

Against this backdrop Sen formulated the themes
† of what Elizabeth De Michelis has termed "proto

Modern Yoga," themes that would reappear in the teachings of his most illustrious pupil, Narendranath Datta, the future Swami Vivekananda, as well as twentieth-century yoga gurus like Bangali Baba. Fundamental to this system was the assumption that the Indian mind had an exceptional innate capacity for Yoga. In Sen's words,

> We Hindus are specially endowed with, and distinguished for, the yoga faculty, which is nothing but this power of spiritual communion and absorption. This faculty, which we have inherited from our forefathers, enables us to annihilate space and time.[3]

While still in his late teens, Vivekananda stayed as a guest in Sen's ashram. It was also Sen who first introduced him to Ramakrishna in 1881, and Sen whom Vivekananda would come to emulate in matters of both substance and style. A product of the intellectual and cultural foment of the colonial capital, the Kolkata-born Vivekananda was a man of his time and place, and in many respects embodied the late nineteenth-century synergy between European and Indian thought. Although he would repudiate the Brahmo Samaj later in life, he was in every respect an heir to its legacy, and in particular to Sen's social ideals and Neo-Vedanta teachings. Other influences that shaped the young Vivekananda were his years of schooling under both Bengali and British mentors, who trained him in traditional Sanskrit scholarship but who also introduced him to the writings of Hegel, Schopenhauer, Darwin, and others.

Following Sen's death in 1884, Vivekananda and other members of the Brahmo Samaj's inner circle gravitated toward Ramakrishna, a Tantric devotee of the goddess Kali living on a Kolkata cremation ground. Although Vivekananda's relationship with this charismatic teacher was brief, cut short by Ramakrishna's death in 1886, it must have been particularly intense, because nearly all that Vivekananda did or said throughout the rest of his short life he attributed to his illustrious guru. Then began a six-year period of wandering, during which Vivekananda, wearing the robes of a Hindu holy man, crisscrossed the Indian subcontinent in a quest for wisdom, but also for the financial backing that would enable him to further spread the gospel of Hindu reform and social uplift, the legacy of his Brahmo Samaj background.

In the hope of raising the funds that had eluded him in his Indian travels, Vivekananda set sail for the United States in 1893. There, his powerful demeanor, charismatic oratory style, and gospel of India's spiritual superiority quickly attracted a following of "New Age" Americans already predisposed to embrace as authentic any teaching coming from the lips of a master from the East. Vivekananda burst onto the world stage through what was by all accounts a bravura series of lectures on Indian spirituality delivered at the World Parliament of Religions, held in Chicago in September of 1893. In the space of seventeen days, he thundered forth a dozen times before growing crowds, dressed in his signature flaming red robes and pale yellow turban. An overnight media sensation, he quickly embarked on a series of lecture tours that would keep him in the United States for nearly all of the following three years. During those years, he would come to absorb many of † the ideas in vogue in the metaphysical milieus in which he found himself, including harmonial religion, Mesmerism, spiritualism, and the occult. These concepts—many of which he had earlier been exposed to during his Kolkata student days through the Freemasons, Theosophists, Unitarians, and other groups—began to appear with increasing frequency in Vivekananda's lectures and writings, which he shrewdly adjusted to the sensitivities and worldview of his spiritually inclined Western audiences. A lecture at Harvard's Graduate † Philosophical Club in May 1896 so impressed William James, the renowned psychologist of religion, that James invited him to chair Harvard's new department of Eastern Philosophy. James also introduced Vivekananda to his brother, the eminent novelist Henry James, who in turn drew the great teacher into the salons of the leading socialites of the time, in Boston, New York, and London. His circle of friends and admirers included Leo Tolstoy, Gertrude Stein, John D. Rockefeller, and Sarah Bernhardt.

In the summer of 1894, Vivekananda added practi- † cal yoga instruction to his teaching curriculum. He appears to have been driven by three motives. The first of these was popular demand. In the United States, Vive-

† kananda quickly became aware of a craving among members of his growing flock for authentic personal experience. For decades the spiritualist and metaphysical milieu had been clamoring for *practical* instruction in the techniques that could put them in touch with the likes of Madame Blavatsky's Himalayan Masters, or, failing that, their own transcendent inner Self. In such circles, Yoga was an idea (and a practice) whose

† time had come. Vivekananda's second motive was more far-reaching. In the months following his electrifying performance at the Parliament of Religions, he came to realize that his time in the West could be put to a dual purpose: in addition to financing the humanitarian work he had planned for India, he would also establish Vedanta centers throughout the United

† States. Accordingly, he founded the Vedanta Society in New York in 1895 and the Ramakrishna Mission in India in 1897: both continue to thrive to the present day. Finally, Vivekananda seized upon Yoga sans yogis as an ideal platform for his Neo-Vedanta agenda, as an ancient Indian science that was spiritual yet divorced from the benighted trappings of the Hindu religion he was seeking to reform. To his credit, Vivekananda's nationalism with respect to Yoga was Indian and not

† Hindu. In recent years, the tides have changed, with Hindu nationalists, as well as such self-appointed culture brokers as Subhash Kak and David Frawley, proclaiming the specifically Hindu roots not only of Yoga but also of world civilization and of all that is good in man.

If the Theosophists put Yoga and yoga on the map of late nineteenth-century urban Indian culture, Vivekananda did so for the rest of the cosmopolitan world through his 1896 book *The Raja Yoga*, which became an overnight classic. Written in two parts, the book comprises a transcription of Vivekananda's lectures † and practical instruction on yoga from the winter of 1895/96, together with a free English translation and commentary on the *Yoga Sutra*, also transcribed from a series of public talks.

Vivekananda's *Raja Yoga* marks a major turning point in the history of *Yoga Sutra* commentary. To begin, it ended a long hiatus during which, for reasons we have seen, no commentaries faithful to Patanjali's work had been written. This was both an opportunity and a liability for Vivekananda. On the one hand, he was freed from the traditional strictures that a flourishing philosophical school would have placed upon a new commentator: respect for a lineage of teachers and their teachings, attention to commentarial conventions, and so forth. He could apply his own powers of reason to the text, improvise, inject nontraditional elements into his analysis—and, following the † lead of Rammohun Roy, adopt Western means of self-representation. But such opportunities also carried risks. Without a support network of living exponents of Yoga philosophy to fall back on, Vivekananda had few means to verify or corroborate his interpretations of Patanjali's work or its commentarial tradition. And so his success came at a heavy price: the severing of the

Yoga Sutra from its original cultural and historical context.

Most important, Vivekananda's *Raja Yoga* was the first English-language work to present itself as a "commentary" on the *Yoga Sutra*. Even when it diverged from commentarial standards, something it did frequently, it's formal presentation—of a line of sutra followed by several lines, paragraphs, or pages of commentary—gave his work the trappings of classical models. The language of Vivekananda's translation and commentary—the language of Neo-Vedanta that has been carried forward into the many "New Age" contexts of modern yoga—was before all else the language of Western science (or scientism) and the pseudo-scientific language of Western spiritualism. As a culture broker, this was Vivekananda's means to modernizing the *Yoga Sutra*'s teachings, to making them relevant for turn-of-the-century North America. This, too, would explain the resounding success of his *Raja Yoga* in the West: it was, at bottom, a self-help book grounded in *Western* esotericism, but because it was the work of an Indian, its Western readership read it as an authentic work of *Eastern* philosophy, on the "Science of Yoga."

For all of these reasons, Vivekananda's *Raja Yoga* was something totally new. A bold, modern fusion of Yoga philosophy and Western science, religion, and the occult, this earnest and impassioned effort to make Indian thought accessible to Western audiences often succeeded at the expense of accuracy. Yet because of his place and prestige as a pioneer Indian prophet to the West, Vivekananda's appropriation of Patanjali's work set the die for much of what has followed down to the present day. Mark Singleton puts the matter succinctly. What Vivekananda did, that none had done before, was to present Raja Yoga "as the *summum bonum* of the (authentic, practical) Indian spiritual tradition. Largely thanks to his efforts, yoga was refashioned as a cultural symbol, in harmony with the religious and intellectual aspirations of educated Indians—but also . . . shot through with Western influences and standards."[4] More than this, Yoga philosophy was for Vivekananda an ideal platform from which to assert the antiquity and superiority of Indian science over that of the West, of Hinduism over Christianity, and, at the same time, to finance his many projects through the income that his lectures and writing on Yoga afforded him. Thanks to the brilliant success and prestige of *Raja Yoga*, the *Yoga Sutra* became the first work of Indian philosophy to garner a wide international readership. Once an orphan in its own land, no other work of Indian philosophy has ever known such a host of adoptive non-Indian parents.

On the basis of his correspondence, we know that Vivekananda wrote his translation and commentary on the *Yoga Sutra* over a matter of months during the first half of 1896. Given his proficiency in Sanskrit, his great powers of memory, and a devoted stenographer to do the writing, this would have been entirely feasible. He wrote the volume while living in New York,

lecturing from it as the writing progressed. It is clear
† from his now published early teachings on Yoga from
1894 that he had previously given very little thought to
the *Yoga Sutra*, and it is interesting to note that when,
in late 1895, he placed his order with an agent in England for the reference works he would use in writing
† *Raja Yoga*, the *Yoga Sutra* was not included in his list
of requests. Rather, he requested a copy of the *Kurma
Purana*, the *Samkhya Karika*, two works on Hatha
Yoga ("Shiva's Collection" and the "Little Lamp"), and
"any other books on Yoga." In another 1895 letter, he
indicated that he was reading the *Yoga Sutra*[s] and "all
the commentators along with them,"[5] but we have no
record of what his actual sources were.

Because his commentary bears little resemblance to
classical models, we may assume that Vivekananda ultimately decided against reading "all the commentators" in the course of his sixth-month sprint to publish
his *Raja Yoga*. Instead, it appears that he did a great
deal of free associating in his work, relying on his own
extensive background knowledge of the Puranas, Indian philosophy, and perhaps Bhoja's commentary and
the *Samkhya Karika* for certain specific matters of
doctrine. His translation (actually, a paraphrase) and
commentary are written in the conversational, and in
some places chatty, pedagogical style of his lectures, a
clear break with the rhetorical complexity of classical
commentarial style but not so far from that of Judge's
lightweight 1888 "interpretation." Of equal importance for the modern history of the *Yoga Sutra* was Vi-

vekananda's idiosyncratic adaptation of the classical commentarial format. Like the classical commentators, he presented each sutra separately together with his interpretation, but unlike them, he did so without referring to the commentaries of Vyasa or any of the other classical authors. In the 120 years that have followed, dozens of self-styled commentators have followed Vivekananda's lead, adhering to commentarial format in churning out volume upon volume of non-classical and often uninformed opinion, drowning the twenty or so original Indian commentaries in an ocean of (mainly) non-Indian "expertise."

Raja Yoga is divided into two parts, the first being an introduction to Patanjali's eight-part practice and the second a translation and commentary on the entire *Yoga Sutra*. Part one, which comprises transcripts of his 1895–96 lectures, is a palimpsest of the many non-Indian influences that contributed to Vivekananda's understanding of Yoga philosophy. Here we see our missionary of Neo-Vedanta working to explore the possible meanings that Patanjali's work could hold for late nineteenth-century seekers. It is also here that we see Vivekananda following the lead of the Puranas, Hatha Yoga sources, and the pandit lore of his day in identifying the *Yoga Sutra* as "the highest authority on Raja-Yoga, and . . . its textbook."[6]

Although he refused membership into the Theosophical Society, there can be no doubt that Vivekananda was influenced by its doctrines, as well perhaps as by its positions on Yoga. Like the Theosophists,

† Vivekananda made Yoga philosophy the keystone of his project of religious reform in India and the gospel of Eastern spirituality that he brought to the materialist West. In many respects, the Theosophists' and Vivekananda's projects were mirror images of each other. For whereas Madame Blavatsky had earlier grafted Indian terminology and concepts onto Western spiritualism and occultism, Vivekananda grafted terminology and concepts from Western spiritualism and scientism onto Indian spirituality and Neo-Vedanta philosophy. The Theosophical teachings turned out to be far more successful in India than in the West, while Vivekananda's lectures and writing have had their most lasting impact in the United States and Europe.

Nowhere is the influence of Theosophical spiritualism more apparent than in Vivekananda's discussion of prana, to which he devotes several pages in both parts one and two of his *Raja Yoga*. If Vivekananda did not take his leads directly from Madame Blavatsky, he may have done so indirectly through his reading of the society's 1893 translation of the "Little Lamp," one of the volumes he had ordered from London in 1895. In her 1885 *Secret Doctrine*, Blavatsky had begun to associate "prana" with both the omnipresent ether of ancient Greek philosophy and the magnetic fluid of Mesmerism and harmonial religion. The Theosophist Shrinivasa Iyangar, in his translation of the "Little Lamp," had
† followed her lead by explicitly differentiating "prana" from breath: " 'Breath' does not mean the air taken in and breathed out, but the Prana, i.e., the magnetic cur-

rent of breath."[7] Vivekananda took matters several steps further, making prana and akasha (a Sanskrit term often translated as "ether") the foundations of a novel metaphysics that owed more to Aristotle and Mesmer than to ancient Indian traditions.

By recasting prana in the way he did, Vivekananda was able to simultaneously dismiss what he called the "queer breathing exercises of the Hatha Yoga" as inau- † thentic, and repackage Western spiritualism as a brand of Raja Yoga. Forcing such straightforward Indian † concepts into a Western occultist mold was, as Elizabeth De Michelis has shown, a deliberate strategy on his part. Like his American audiences, Vivekananda was influenced by the Theosophists and deeply engaged in the alternative healing traditions that characterized the "New Thought" of the period. In his expansive reworking of the yogic principles and practices of breath control, we see him speaking their language, a language that many modern yoga gurus continue to speak. Unaware of how fast and loose Vivekananda was playing with these Indian philosophical concepts, some of the great scientific minds of his time were highly impressed by his ability to shuttle between modern "Eastern" spirituality and modern Western scientific theory. Nikola Tesla, who was introduced to † Vivekananda by Sarah Bernhardt, would cite him in his pioneering research on electromagnetism, precisely on the topics of prana and akasha.

Like the majority of nonspecialist readers of the *Yoga Sutra*, Vivekananda was unclear about the history of the interactions between the distinct fields of Raja Yoga, Hatha Yoga, and Tantric Yoga. Time and again, in both parts of his book, he refers to features of the yogic body—the three major channels, the seven chakras or lotuses—that have no place in the *Yoga Sutra* but which are leitmotivs of Tantric Yoga. A schematic drawing of the same yogic body, inserted into the "Psychic Prana" chapter of *Raja Yoga*, is entirely based on Hatha Yoga traditions. So too, his explanation of the breathing exercises of pranayama—the fourth component of the eight-part practice—as well as the awakening of the serpentine energy called kundalini, and the effects of holding the breath for extended durations, are found in the Puranas, Tantras, and Hatha Yoga works, but not in the *Yoga Sutra*.

In spite of this, Vivekananda missed no occasion to denigrate Hatha Yoga as inferior and counterproductive to the practice of his so-called Raja Yoga. There can be little doubt that his negative evaluation of Hatha Yoga flowed from its identification with the practices of India's yogis. For the many reasons we have already seen, the yogi lifestyle epitomized the benighted, corrupted forms of Hinduism that Vivekananda, as an heir to the Romantics, was attempting to reform. Like them, he was seeking to recover the pristine origins of the Hindu religion—"nuggets of gold and truth"[8] as he called them, from the "masses of superstition" under which they were buried. In this, Vivekananda joined a chorus of voices that viewed India's yogis as the modern-day bearers of the ancient tradition of the true Yoga, Raja Yoga, but who had, out of ignorance and perfidy, allowed it to become eclipsed by Hatha practices and antisocial ways. This he states in no uncertain terms in his first chapter of part one:

> Mystery-mongering weakens the human brain. It †
> has well-nigh destroyed Yoga—one of the grand-
> est of sciences. From the time it was discovered,
> more than four thousand years ago, Yoga was per-
> fectly delineated, formulated, and preached in
> India. It is a striking fact that the more modern the
> commentator the greater the mistakes he makes,
> while the more ancient the writer the more ratio-
> nal he is. Most of the modern writers talk of all
> sorts of mystery. Thus Yoga fell into the hands of a
> few persons who made it a secret, instead of letting
> the full blaze of daylight and reason fall upon it.
> They did so that they might have the powers to
> themselves.[9]

In fairness to Vivekananda, it should be noted that his own guru Ramakrishna had been ambiguous in his ap- †
preciation of Hatha Yoga. On the one hand, he had praised Raja as superior to Hatha, yet, when describing the actual practice of yoga, he spoke in terms of awak-ening and raising the kundalini through the lotuses or chakras. Another of Vivekananda's likely influences was one of his mentors from his student days in Kolk-ata. This was the Bengali intellectual Ishwar Chandra †
Vidyasagar, who shared his own 1853 English-language translation of Madhava's "Compendium" with the

young Vivekananda. As we have seen, this work, which was held in great esteem among Indian reformers, featured in its long chapter on "Patanjali's System" several elements of Hatha and Tantric Yoga. Another of Vidyasagar's projects would also have a powerful impact on the modern history of Yoga philosophy. In † 1850 a report he submitted to the secretary to the Council of Education in Kolkata requested that the Sanskrit College there broaden its instruction in philosophy to include, among other texts, the *Yoga Sutra*. It was here that several decades later Hariharananda Aranya, arguably the most important Indian *Yoga Sutra* commentator of the twentieth century, first received instruction in Yoga philosophy.

† Vivekananda's reliance on the Puranas over and against the *Yoga Sutra* itself is exemplified in the use he makes of the *Kurma Purana*, inasmuch as he concludes part one of his *Raja Yoga* with "a summary of Raja-yoga freely translated from the *Kurma Purana*." Here again we see Vivekananda presenting data culled from a hodgepodge of sources as "Raja Yoga" and identifying that Raja Yoga with Patanjali's teachings. Vivekananda's expurgated version of the *Kurma*'s chapter on the eight-part practice is noteworthy on a number † of points. To begin, the *Kurma*'s account, while paying lip service to the techniques of the eight-part practice (but without mentioning either Patanjali or the *Yoga Sutra*), is essentially a guide to yogic meditation on Shiva in his multiple aspects and forms, culminating in either identity or union with the great God. In this re-

spect, it is like several other Puranic accounts of the Yoga system: a summary of the eight-part practice and a definition of Yoga as union with God. When one looks at the unexpurgated *Kurma* chapter, however, one finds that only thirty-four of its 146 verses treat of the eight-part practice or, for that matter, any form of yoga that could possibly be identified with the "Raja Yoga" of the *Yoga Sutra*.

In fact, the term that the *Kurma* uses for this type of yoga is not "Raja," but rather "Abhava" ("Absence," "Negation"), which it casts as a markedly inferior form of practice in comparison with the Mahayoga ("Great Yoga") of identification with Shiva. At one point, the *Kurma* identifies this latter form of yoga as "Pashupata Yoga," the yoga of the ancient Pashupata order of Shaiva ascetics who were the forerunners of the widely despised yogis. Vivekananda translates the chapter in a highly selective way, by leaving out nearly every verse not devoted to the eight-part practice—as well as every one of the chapter's frequent references to Shiva—and by inserting near the end of his chapter a quote from the *Bhagavad Gita*.

In his introduction to part two of *Raja Yoga*, in which he seeks to present a sweeping overview of the *Yoga Sutra* in its broader philosophical context, we once again see Vivekananda writing in the familiar Vedanta mode: "The goal is to manifest this Divinity within, by controlling nature, external and internal."[10] In the balance of part two, the remarks Vivekananda offers in his commentary on the *Yoga Sutra* aphorisms are generally respectful of the text. At times, however, his interpretations are highly forced, breaking with commentarial tradition even as they allow him to underscore the superiority and scientific nature of ancient Hindu thought. A lucid study by Dermot Killingley of two of the opening verses of Patanjali's fourth chapter shall serve as a case in point. A straightforward translation of the terse Sanskrit of those sutras reads as follows:

> Change of species [results] from the filling in of their [inherent] natures. (4.2)
> The efficient cause is not the motor of these [changes of their inherent] natures: only the piercing of the barrier [takes place] through it, as in the case of the farmer. (4.3)

Vivekananda's English "adaptation" of these sutras was quite different:

> The change into another species is by the filling in of Nature. (4.2)
> Good and bad deeds are not the direct cause in the transformations of Nature, but they act as breakers of obstacles to the evolutions of Nature: as a farmer breaks the obstacles to the course of water, which then runs down of its own nature. (4.3)

In his commentary on these verses, Vivekananda betrays the intention behind his insertion of the word "evolutions":

So all progress and power are already in every man;   †
perfection is man's nature. . . . If anyone can take
the bar off, in rushes Nature. . . . It is Nature that is
driving us towards perfection, and eventually she
will bring everyone there. . . . Today the evolution
theory of the ancient Yogis will be better understood in the light of modern research. And yet the
theory of the Yogis is a better explanation. The . . .
causes of evolution advanced by the moderns . . .
are inadequate. . . . But the great ancient evolutionist, Patanjali, declares that the true secret of evolution is the manifestation of the perfection, which is
already in every being. . . . So in man there is the
potential god, kept in by the locks and bars of ignorance. When knowledge breaks these bars, the
god becomes manifest.[11]

Contrary to Vivekananda's reading, these sutras were
not concerned with collective species but rather with
individual persons who stand an equal chance of rising
or falling along the great chain of being when they are
reborn. Vivekananda, however, chose to view them as
evocations of a straight-line evolution of the human
race toward an innate preselected perfection. This was
a spiritual process: there was a Spirit present in all be-   †
ings, and the full self-manifestation of that divine
Spirit, that transcendent Self, was the teleological purpose of evolution. The Brahmo Samaj position that the
scientific knowledge of the ancient Hindus had yet to
be fathomed by Western science is also clearly present

here, in Vivekananda's argument for the superiority of Patanjali's evolutionary theory over that of Darwin. Modern yoga gurus who have followed Vivekananda's lead include Bhagwan Rajneesh (a.k.a. Osho), who in 1984 credited Patanjali with having, "for the first time in the history of humanity . . . brought religion to the state of science: he made religion a science; bare laws; no belief is needed."[12]

† Vivekananda was so taken with his readings of these two sutras that he repeated them on four different occasions. On one of these, he identified evolutionary progress with the enhanced control of the body attained through Yoga. On another, he pushed his argument further, maintaining that this doctrine of inherent perfection is "the great difference between Eastern and Western thought," even as he attacked "such awful doctrines as that we are all born sinners."[13] As powerful a rhetorical position as this may have been for his late nineteenth-century audiences, it was utterly at odds with the original purport of these sutras and classical Indian commentaries on their subject. Here, an overview of that history is instructive, because it offers a window into the worldviews and modus operandi of India's classical schoolmen. As we have seen, these commentators approached their subjects in much the same way as the judicial review process. This was not the place for flashy innovation; rather, the goal was to demonstrate how the concept under examination fit into the broader picture of universal knowledge.

By interpreting these two sutras in the way he did, Vivekananda excised them from their context, in this case verses one to six of the fourth chapter, which were treated as a coherent whole by both Patanjali and his classical commentators. Patanjali introduces his discussion in the first sutra, which posits that the supernatural powers of Yoga that had been the subject of the preceding chapter arise through a number of transformations, of which the most common is rebirth. If a man is reborn as a bird, he suddenly becomes possessed of a power of flight that he had not enjoyed in his previous life. However, Patanjali and his commentators also hypothesized that one could also be reborn as a *human* possessed of the supernatural powers of flight and so forth, due to the effects of one's karma, one's prior acts. The two verses that follow, the verses upon which Vivekananda based his commentary on "evolution," explain just how such transformations or reconfigurations—from one body to another—occur, not only through rebirth but also, in rare cases, within the course of a single lifetime.

The classical commentators, beginning with Vyasa, provide examples from Hindu mythology to elucidate these verses, evoking the brahmin Nandishvara who, through his pious acts, was changed into a god while still alive, and a king named Nahusha whose overweening pride instantaneously transformed him into a serpent. Just as when a barrier has been lifted or broken to allow water to move from one field to another, they tell us, the merits or demerits of human acts and intentions can remove the obstacles that stand in the way of their *immediate* transformation into other types of beings. The merits and demerits are not the direct or efficient cause of the changes any more than the farmer who pierces the barrier of an irrigation canal himself causes the water to flow. Rather, in the same way that he simply unblocks the sole impediment to the force of gravity upon the mass of water, so too a creature's merits and demerits remove the obstacles that stand in the way of its change into a member of another species.

The three verses that follow—*Yoga Sutra* 4.4–6—concern the yogi who is capable of creating and assuming several bodies simultaneously, even as he continues to inhabit his own body. For both Patanjali and the classical commentators, the connection was clear: the yogi possessed of such supernatural powers is a special case of the transformation of one type of creature into another, in this case from a singular being (the yogi) into multiple beings (the many bodies he assumes or inhabits). Under such circumstances, the question that arises, and which Patanjali next answers, concerns the relationship between the mind of the meditating yogi and the many bodies he inhabits: do they have individual minds or one mind? And, if the latter, is that one mind the same as or different from the mind of the yogi who inhabits these other bodies even as he remains "himself"? Patanjali's response is that while each constructed body is possessed of its own mind, those multiple minds remain subject to the yogi's own ego

and will. By way of example, Bhoja evokes the sparks a †
fire throws up: the individual minds are so many "scintillations" of the dominant mind that controls them.
Vijnanabhikshu cites the case the mind of the epic hero †
Rama: although he was the incarnation of the omniscient god Vishnu, his individual "human" mind nonetheless remained unaware of his inherent divinity.

Hariharananda Aranya uses the example of a hypnotist. Just as the magician's mind acts on the minds †
of his spectators to produce mass hypnosis, so the yogi's dominant mind controls the secondary minds in
the bodies he has created. For Aranya, these verses further suggest the way that Ishvara, the fully liberated
"Master of Yoga," could use his created mind to "favor
those who are qualified for liberation" at the end of a
cosmic cycle. In a similar vein, Vachaspati Mishra and †
Vijnanabhikshu both quote a verse from the Puranas,
which states that "by virtue of his authoritative power,
the Ishvara, though one, becomes many. Then being
many he becomes one. And from him also proceed
all these variations of consciousness."[14] Both also quote
a passage from the *Mahabharata*, which describes
human masters of yoga as creating or taking over multiple bodies, using some to enjoy the pleasures of the
world and others to practice asceticism. All of these
may be drawn back into the yogi's own body and mind
"like the sun does with its rays of light." †

The power of the yogi to create, take over, and con †
trol other bodies and minds was universally accepted,
not only among Yoga philosophers but also in nearly

every philosophical school, religious sect, and written tradition of medieval India. Exponents of Nyaya-Vaisheshika philosophy, the great Advaita Vedanta philosopher Shankara, as well as a variety of Shaivas, Buddhists, and Jains all assumed that these yogic powers were real. A rich mythology predating the *Yoga Sutra*, and going back to the Hindu *Mahabharata* and *Maitri Upanishad* and the Buddhist *Vimuttimagga*, portrayed yogis in these roles, and commentators cited these and other sources as scriptural precedents for their philosophical analyses. Some applied the principles set forth in these three sutras to resolve philosophical conundrums found in other works. How, for example, could Krishna assert in the *Bhagavad Gita* (4.37) that through the practice of Yoga, one's "fire of knowledge" would instantaneously burn away the karma accumulated in thousands of previous lives? Because, as the ninth-century Nyaya philosopher Vyomashiva explained, a yogi could use all the minds in all the bodies he had created or appropriated as a great karma-burning machine. Vivekananda—who did not wish to remind his readers of the links between the *Yoga Sutra* and India's yogis, and who, following the Neo-Vedanta strategy of employing his own powers of reason over and against commentarial convention—placed his own authority above his august predecessors and misappropriated these verses into a late nineteenth-century sermon on evolutionary theory.

By using the methods of European classicists, Henry Thomas Colebrooke recovered the *Yoga Sutra* from

oblivion and made its content known to the nascent field of Western Indology. By adopting the teachings of the Puranas and pandits, and by using the methods and concepts of European and American spiritualists, Swami Vivekananda recovered the *Yoga Sutra* from oblivion and made its content known to the milieus of Western spiritualism. Over the past century, Vivekananda's legacy has prevailed in the yoga subculture, where teachers continue to confuse Yoga philosophy with Puranic, Hatha, and Tantric doctrines; to present Western metaphysical and scientistic concepts in Indian trappings; to identify Yoga as a healing tradition; to assert the scientific foundations of Yoga; and to present Raja as the highest form of Yoga. If, to again quote Mark Singleton, "the vision of the *Yoga Sutra* as the source of a timeless tradition of Classical Indian Yoga is but an *idée reçue* of the modern era,"[15] there †
can be no doubt that Vivekananda was its primary transmitter.

The *Yoga Sutra* in the Muslim World

In 1893, the same year that Vivekananda sailed west into history, a north Indian Sufi master (pir) from the Naqshbandi order initiated two young Hindu brothers with the understanding that one of them would become his successor. When the old pir died, the elder of the two, Ramachandra Chaudhari became Mahatma Ramchandraji Maharaj, cosharer of the office of pir with his master's brother. At once a Hindu householder, the master of a Muslim religious order, a tax collector for the British Raj, and a budding yoga practitioner, Ramachandra founded a school that he would later call Ananda Yoga ("Yoga of Beatitude") in the first decade of the twentieth century.

Although Ramachandra had first been initiated into yoga practice by a Hindu holy man named Swami Brahmananda while still in his youth, legend has it that his authority to teach his new form of yoga to both Hindus and Muslims arose out of an experience he had had two years prior to his 1893 Sufi initiation. One eve-

†

ning, while on his way home from his workplace, a violent thunderstorm broke out just as he was passing by his future master's madrasa. Seeing that his clothes were soaked, the Sufi master covered Ramachandra, the future Hindu Mahatma, with a warm quilt.

> Then the Mahatma all of a sudden lost his senses, and without hesitation the Maulawi disclosed his entire spiritual wealth through a flight of subtle energy (shakti-pat) to the heart of Ramcandraji, thus fulfilling the wishes of his own venerable master ... according to whom one day a Hindu boy would come to meet the Shah who was to bestow this Divine knowledge on him, since this science originally belonged to the Hindus.[1]

This hagiographical account, remarkable in its ecumenism, instructs all who have ears to hear that ancient Hindu wisdom was transmitted by a Muslim master to a Hindu disciple, via the Tantric technique of shakti-pat, in order that that disciple impart said knowledge to Hindus and Muslims alike. And this is what Ramchandraji did, offering instruction in a blend of meditational techniques, Hatha Yoga, and such Sufi practices as visualization (muraqaba) and "the science hidden in the breast" (ilm-i-sina). Because his day job as tax collector often took him on the road, he was able to devote his evenings to instruction to a growing circle of followers, and so Ananda Yoga quickly spread across north India's Gangetic heartland.

A series of successors furthered the expansion of Ananda Yoga, which today counts some 100,000 adherents across India and around the world. Over the past four decades, the formal links between Ananda Yoga and the Naqshbandi order have fallen away, and while relations between the two groups have remained cordial, the language of yoga that Ananda Yoga and its offshoots employ has become increasingly Hinduized. This has especially been the case with the Sahaj Marg, an international offshoot of Ananda Yoga, which has expressly replaced Sufi terminology with cognate terms from the *Yoga Sutra*, identified in its teachings as Raja Yoga.

The Islamic embrace of things yogic has not been limited to India. Yoga has been popular across the Muslim world for several decades, with yoga centers thriving in countries across the Middle East—including in Iran, without interference from the Iranian theocracy. However, in recent years, the beast of identity politics has reared its ugly head, with an outright ban on yoga that the government of Malaysia issued (and quickly lifted) in November of 2008, and a fatwa against Muslims practicing yoga that Indonesian clerics emitted two months later. In both cases, it was the perceived Hindu content of yoga practice that was judged anathema to the true Islamic faith. Muslim ideologues have not held the monopoly on religious intolerance, however. In 1989, Cardinal Ratzinger, the future Pope Benedict, warned Catholics of the dangers

of "non-Christian forms of meditation" while challenging Hindu Nondualist metaphysics from the
standpoint of Catholic theology. More recently, Chris- †
tian fundamentalist personalities like Pat Robertson
and Albert Mohler have inveighed against yoga practice by members of their flock, arguing that using the
body as a vehicle for achieving consciousness of the divine undercuts one's commitment to Christ, or that by
repeating the names of Hindu gods while practicing
yoga, Christians are implicitly denying the one true
God. Similar arguments have been used in attempts to
prohibit the teaching of yoga in physical education
classes in public schools. For its part, the Hindu America Foundation has initiated a "Take Back Yoga" infor- †
mational campaign aimed at restoring the yoga
"brand" to its Hindu source.

It may be argued that these three fundamentalist
constituencies—Muslim, Christian, and Hindu—
have seized upon Yoga as a symbol for all things
Hindu. In the face of globalization and other forces
they can no longer control, fundamentalist leaders
have sought to defend the purity of their respective
traditions by demonizing (or glorifying, in the case of
the Hindus) the wildly successful yoga subculture. In
these times of institutionalized bigotry, it is difficult to
imagine that things could ever have been otherwise.
Yet on the Christian side, Michel Sage, who authored †
the first French translation of the *Yoga Sutra* in 1921,
was a devout Catholic who nonetheless embraced
such unauthorized doctrines as the reincarnation of

the soul and the laws of karma, without being disciplined by the Church. One of the most sensitive and sympathetic works on Yoga philosophy was authored by the Jesuit Gaspar Koelmans, and a "Christian" reading of the *Yoga Sutra* has recently been proposed by a member of the south India–based Carmelites of the Mary Immaculate congregation.

In the Muslim world as well, there have been times when theologians and culture brokers have not embraced the citadel mentality so prevalent today. Two cases worth noting both hark back to periods in which Islam was politically dominant, or rising to dominance, in South Asia. The latter half of the sixteenth century, the apogee of the Mughal Empire in India, was marked by the long rule of its greatest emperor, Akbar. The third in a line of Central Asian conquerors who traced their Timurid lineage back to Tamerlane and Genghis Khan, Akbar consolidated and expanded Mughal rule across nearly all of India, ushering in an era of peace and prosperity. The form of Islam the Timurids had brought to India from their Iranian homeland was Shi'ism, a markedly mystical strain of † the faith compared to Sunni orthodoxy. That mystic heritage had a strong effect on Akbar, who had from a very early age also found inspiration in the teachings of such Persian Sufi mystics as Rumi, Hafiz, and others, and who progressively abandoned the ways of Sunni Islam over the course his long reign.

† We can trace this trend back to 1573, when Akbar began to consider a proposition made by a heretical

theologian named Shaikh Mubarak that he be declared infallible in matters of religion, thereby establishing himself as the imperial head of both church and state. This was enacted in 1579 with the "Infallibility Decree," but things had already come to a head five years earlier when Akbar had formally renounced Islam and proclaimed a new faith of his own, called the "Divine Religion." The high priest of the new imperial creed was Shaikh Mubarak's son Abu'l Fazl, who remained Akbar's closest ally and confidant throughout the latter half of his long reign.

With Akbar's new religion came a policy of religious tolerance with regard to his many non-Muslim subjects (Hindus, Jains, Zoroastrians, and Christians), coupled with a persecution of Muslims, most particularly the orthodox Sunnis who staunchly opposed his innovations. In fact, many of these new policies were of Abu'l Fazl's own making, as was a novel imperial ideology that elevated Akbar to the level of a god on earth. These radical new ideas were woven into Abu'l †
Fazl's two greatest works, the *Akbar Nama* ("Life of Akbar"), a sweeping chronicle of Akbar's forty-seven-year reign, and the far more readable *Ain-i Akbari* ("Institutes of Akbar"), an imperial survey and manual for government.

Here, by way of legitimating the emperor's infallibility and divine right to rule, Abu'l Fazl traced Akbar's lineage back to Adam, and—via a virgin mother impregnated by a ray of divine light—to a series of conquerors including Genghis Khan, Tamerlane, and

Akbar's grandfather Babur, the founder of the Mughal Empire. Taking his inspiration from a mystic Persian strain of Neoplatonist philosophy, Abu'l Fazl also asserted that Akbar was possessed of a divine effulgence, which, transmitted through the angel Gabriel, afforded him greater esoteric knowledge and authority than not only the Sharia jurists, but also the most saintly Sufi masters, as well as the eagerly awaited Mahdi, the Shi'a Messiah. That same supernatural charisma and wisdom also caused the holy men of other Indian traditions, including the yogis, to gravitate toward Akbar's imperial person. In this last case, the attraction was mutual, with Akbar often visiting and holding forth with Hindu holy men, and even building a "City of Yogis" for them on the outskirts of the city of Agra.

An Indian "Mirror of Kings," Abu'l Fazl's "Institutes" stands as an encyclopedic account of every aspect of Akbar's realm, from its physical and human resources to its indigenous systems of knowledge. As such, much of the fourth book of his work is devoted to the six Hindu philosophical systems, concluding with a short disquisition on Patanjali's school, which comprises an erudite synopsis of the *Yoga Sutra* as both a metaphysical treatise and a blueprint for a type of psychological training. Although Abu'l Fazl relied heavily upon the Hindu pandits for his data, his greatest challenge was to translate Hindu concepts and Sanskrit terms into an Islamic idiom. So, for example, referring to sutra 3.51, he defines a person who has reached the second "honey stage" of yogic practices as one who "effaces rust from the mirror of the heart,"[2] an expression foreign to Hindu parlance. On the subject † of celibacy, one of the inner restraints of the eight-part practice, his expression that the practitioner "must also avoid the society of women lest his brain be distracted and melancholy ensue"[3] appears to have originated entirely from Abu'l Fazl's own brain. On the other hand, his use of the Persian equivalent of the Sanskrit aish- † varya ("mastery") to denote the occult powers that are the topic of much of the *Yoga Sutra*'s third chapter probably drew upon the Shaiva and Vaishnava traditions of his pandit informants, since it is not found in either the *Yoga Sutra* or its commentarial literature.

In his discussion of asana, the third component of the eight-part practice, Abu'l Fazl numbers the pos- † tures at eighty-four, a canonical number from the late Hatha Yoga traditions that were so prevalent in his time, but not found in the *Yoga Sutra*. Clearly sharing Akbar's fascination with India's yogis, he also demonstrates his familiarity with broader yogic traditions concerning breath control and the "subtle body," concluding his overview with a show of admiration that testifies to his own open-mindedness with regard to non-Islamic traditions:

> The ascetics of this country can so hold their †
> breath that they will breathe but once in twelve
> years. . . . Although this language may seem incred
> ible in the eyes of those affected by the taint of nar-

row custom, those who acknowledge the wonderful power of God will find in it no cause of astonishment.[4]

Akbar and Abu'l Fazl were not the last Mughals to be attracted to India's yoga traditions and practitioners. Imperial Mughal interest in Hindu mysticism peaked in the tragic person of Akbar's great-grandson, Dara Shukuh, a weak heir apparent to the throne who was assassinated in 1659 at the order of his notorious younger brother, Aurangzeb. An established Sufi scholar, Dara Shukuh maintained that at the time when the Prophet Muhammad had received the revelations of the Qur'an, he was also engaged in the practice of repeating the name of God (zikr) to the accompaniment of postural practice, breath control, and † concentration. Dara Shukuh called this body of practice the "King of the Zikrs," which as Craig Davis has noted is uncannily similar in several of its details to a particular sequence of Hatha Yoga exercises. The "Little Lamp," a work likely known to Dara Shukuh, ranges these practices under the heading of "Raja Yoga." As Davis suggests, Dara Shukuh may well have named his "King of the Zikrs" after Raja, the so-called King of Yogas. Postures and breath control were not the sole areas of overlap between Sufi and Hindu theory and practice, and Dara Shukuh also drew explicit links between Sufi accounts of the spiritual centers and the † chakras of Tantric Yoga. The Sufi Naqshbandis would further elaborate on these, identifying the inner "centers of light" ('ilm-i-lata'if) of their system with the chakras.

We see traditions such as these being carried forward into the modern age through Ramachandra's late nineteenth-century Naqshbandi pir, but in fact, Islamic interest in India's yoga traditions in general, and the *Yoga Sutra* in particular, predated the imperial Mughals by several centuries. In this regard, the authors of the authoritative *Oxford History of India* note Abu'l Fazl's debt to an Islamic scholar who preceded him by some five hundred years. This was Abu al-Rayhan Muhammad ibn Ahmad al-Biruni—known to the West as Alberuni—whose work titled *Tahqiq-i–Hind* ("India") was "unique in Muslim literature, except in so far as it was imitated without acknowledgement . . . by Abu-l Fazl in the *Ain-i Akbari*."[5]

Born in the city of Gurganj on the shore of the Aral Sea in what would be modern-day Turkmenistan, Alberuni was one of the greatest minds in what S. Frederick Starr has identified as a Central Asian "zone of genius." From 800 to 1100, the principal cities of the region—from Gurganj in the west to Samarkand, Ghazni, and Kashgar in the east—were cosmopolitan centers rivaling the Baghdad of the Abbasid Caliphate for world leadership in the fields of mathematics, chemistry, medicine, astronomy, philosophy, and music. From a very early age, Alberuni enjoyed the support of powerful Central Asian rulers whose patronage allowed him to debate the leading scientific ideas of his day with the greatest lights of the Islamic world: the philosopher Ibn Sina (known to the West as Avicenna) and the Persian poet Firdausi among many others. Then, in his late forties, Alberuni's life changed forever, when he was forcibly exiled from his homeland and installed in the court of Mahmud of Ghazni, who, while a generous patron of the arts and sciences, was also a ruthless autocrat ruling over an ever-expanding empire.

†   A series of military campaigns that Mahmud launched against western India have left an indelible mark on the modern Hindu psyche, such that together with the seventeenth-century Mughal emperor Aurangzeb, Mahmud stands as the perennial poster boy for Islamic plunder and iconoclasm. Operating out of his stronghold in the Hindu Kush, Mahmud began in the year 1000 to mount a series of invasions that took his armies deeper and deeper into the Indian subcontinent, from which he extracted increasingly fabulous spoils of war. His 1026 plunder of the fabulous Somnath Temple of Shiva on the southern coast of the Kathiawar peninsula is the stuff of legend, and accounts of the endless camel caravans that carried the gold and jewels of the temple's treasury out of India have been a major rallying cry of Hindu nationalists for over a century. Mahmud's military campaigns were not limited to the South Asian subcontinent, however. In 1017, his armies conquered Chorasmia and its capital of Gurganj, far to the west. It was on this occasion that Mahmud took Alberuni captive, bringing him back to Ghazni as a spoil of war before posting him

to the Punjab region of modern-day Pakistan for a twelve-year period—sufficient time for him to become an accomplished Sanskritist. There, his observations on Indian life, learning, society, and religion issued in the remarkable volume titled "India."

Alberuni's work is an exceptional window into both high and low Hindu culture of eleventh-century India. Given his own special expertise in astronomy and time reckoning, Alberuni devoted a large portion of his work to a detailed survey of cognate Hindu systems, about which he was generally contemptuous. But Alberuni was also interested in India's philosophical systems, and in this context he has emerged as an important witness to the early history of the *Yoga Sutra*. In his "India," he refers on several occasions to the work, as well as to a commentary he says was translated by his † own hand into the Arabic language. In 1922, while carrying out research in an Istanbul archive, the Islamicist † Louis Massignon stumbled upon Alberuni's lost translation, which had been scrawled in the margins of the manuscript of another unrelated text. His version— † which is cast as a dialogue between Patanjali and an "ascetic roaming in the deserts and the forests"[6]—is of particular interest because it diverges on many points from the extant Sanskrit-language commentaries of its time, and because a number of the sutras contained in Patanjali's "original" work are missing. This and other † data have led some scholars to conclude that the version of the *Yoga Sutra* upon which the commentary translated by Alberuni was based was earlier than the one used by Vyasa, and that that commentary had "probably [been] written at a time when the Bhashya of Vyasa had not yet attained any great sanctity and authority."[7]

Translated into English, Alberuni's Arabic rendering of the commentary's title is the "Book of the Indian Patanjali on Liberation from the Afflictions": critical scholars generally refer to it by the abbreviated name *Kitab Patanjal* ("Patanjali's Book"). The Yoga system presented in this commentary diverges significantly from that of Patanjali's *Yoga Sutra* and Vyasa's "Commentary" inasmuch as it presents union with God as the final goal of Yoga practice. There are two
† possible explanations for this shift. One hypothesis, first broached by the great Bengali historian of Indian philosophy, Surendranath Dasgupta, is that this commentary reflects an authentic modification of Yoga philosophy in its early development and is perhaps the work of a different Patanjali than the author of the *Yoga Sutra* as we know it. A second, and to my mind more plausible, explanation is that Alberuni was influenced by epic and Puranic accounts of Yoga, which, as we have seen, identified Ishvara with either Vishnu or Shiva, and defined Yoga as union with that God.

† Although Alberuni indicates that he was assisted in his translation by Indian schoolmen, there is much that appears to be the product of his own powers of reason and his training in Aristotelian and Islamic phi-
† losophy. So, for example, in translating sutra 2.15, he interprets the Indian philosophical question of what

constitutes the individual self in terms of a central issue of Islamic philosophy: whether the essence of Man is the body or the soul. Unique to Alberuni's version is the inclusion of alchemy (rasayana) as a means to salvation. Elixir alchemy was a cultural fashion in India between the ninth and thirteenth centuries, as Alberuni himself documents in his "India." It is also mentioned in Bhoja's commentary on *Yoga Sutra* 4.1. †

In many places, Alberuni finds himself obliged to coin new technical terms in Arabic to do justice to such Sanskrit concepts as klesa ("taint," "affliction," which he translates as "burden") and buddhi ("intellect," for which he provides the reading of "heart"). Elsewhere, he translates a Sanskrit term denoting nondiscursive intuitive knowledge with a Sufi term for mystical cognition: "the eye of the heart." In the same spirit, he translates the title of the *Yoga Sutra*'s first chapter ("On Pure Contemplation") as "Making the Heart Steadfastly Fixed." Posture (asana) is translated as "quietude," ether is either "air" or "sky," and the Hindu deities (devas) become "angels." The earliest documented *translator* of the *Yoga Sutra*, we see Alberuni grappling with the same problems that have beset the many modern scholars, teachers, and dilettantes who have attempted to respect the original intent of its terminology and concepts while translating them into foreign languages and idioms. †

Since the original Sanskrit-language commentary from which Alberuni generated his translation has been lost, we cannot know whether it was structured along the same lines as his version. How to explain the fact, for example, that Alberuni introduces his translation with the discussion of a topic that is only mentioned in sutras 1.7 and 2.45, and which is relatively peripheral to the philosophical preoccupations of the † *Yoga Sutra* and its classical commentaries? This is the topic of the perception or cognition of things hidden from normal sense perception, either due to their minute size, great distance from the viewer in space or time, or the existence of a barrier. This is a theme that receives far greater attention in other schools of Indian philosophy. That it should be given pride of place in Alberuni's commentary is yet another indication that his source may have belonged to an otherwise "lost tradition" in the annals of Yoga philosophy.

Another area in which the commentary Alberuni translated diverges from those of Vyasa and other early schoolmen is its discussion of sutra 3.26, which reads "from perfect discipline of the sun, knowledge of the worlds." Beginning with Vyasa, it had been a commentarial convention to present a traveler's guide to the Cosmic Egg, which contains all of the "worlds" evoked in the sutra. As a result, this sutra was the object of one of the most extensive commentaries of the entire work, because the Cosmic Egg is a mighty egg with many, † many worlds inside of it. This elaborate cosmology had first appeared in its fullness in the Puranas, of which Alberuni was clearly aware, noting in his "India" that his source differed from the latter on several points. It also diverged significantly from Vyasa's commentarial description, all of which leads to the conclusion that the details of the wondrous landscapes of the Cosmic Egg had not yet been entirely standardized by the end of the first millennium of the Common Era. Vyasa concluded his commentary on this sutra by instructing yogis to concentrate on the sun, or on any other cosmic zone, until all of these worlds were clearly seen. This would indicate that his purpose in detailing them was to aid advanced practitioners to visualize those worlds in all their complexity. Unlike Vyasa and later commentators, however, Alberuni's commentary does not contain this final injunction. As was the case in the Puranic traditions, God was the sole proper object of meditation, since He alone was capable of granting salvation to his creatures.

Alberuni concludes his translation by addressing † his Muslim readership on the question of "the impossible (things referred to) in this book." Here, he sounds much like a modern-day professor of comparative religion, evoking the "impossible" nature of the manifest miracles of the Muslim prophets as well as the powers attributed by Christians to the relics of their saints and martyrs. Then, adopting a condescending—or one might say, Hegelian—attitude, he says of the Hindus whose impossible things these are, that they are incapable of distinguishing between science and fantasy.

The *Yoga Sutra* Becomes a Classic

† In his "India," Alberuni tells the story of an alchemical experiment involving an unnamed king that had taken place "in the city of Dhara, the capital of Malava, which is in our days ruled by Bhojadeva."[1] Alberuni's Bhojadeva was none other than King Bhoja, the illustrious author of the "Royal Sun" commentary, and it is an irony of history that the man who had forcibly brought Alberuni to India was later met in battle by an army led by Bhoja himself. That two significant *Yoga Sutra* commentators should have had but one degree of separation in the eleventh century is, if nothing else, an indication of the popularity of Yoga philosophy in this period. The centuries around the turn of the second millennium were the *Yoga Sutra*'s high-water mark, only surpassed by its popularity over the past forty years. In addition to the works of Alberuni and Bhoja, the same period saw the appearance of two other classical commentaries: Vachaspati Mishra's definitive "Expert Guide to the True Principles" and

Shankara's "Exposition of the Commentary on Patanjali's Yoga Teaching" (if the ninth-century Shankara was in fact its author). Two important Jain adaptations of Yoga philosophy also appeared during these centuries, alongside multiple references to the *Yoga Sutra* in Kashmir Shaiva and Tamil Shrivaishnava philosophical works, and the continuing fusion of Yoga philosophy with Tantric Yoga, Hindu devotion, and Vedanta philosophy in early works belonging to the canon of the *Yoga Upanishads*.

The turn of the millennium was also a time of contestation in yogic matters; as we saw in chapter 2, during this period various sectarian groups and philosophical schools began to propose alternate readings of yoga—as "discipline," "meditation," even "union"—in conjunction with the particular forms of theism they were espousing. Alternate readings of the "eight-part practice" were also proposed. The most ecumenical among the Yoga philosophers of the time were the Jains Haribhadra and Hemachandra. While Haribhadra presents several alternate systems of Yoga in his eighth-century *Yogadrishtisamuccaya* ("Collection of Views on Yoga"), the *Yoga Sutra* served as what Christopher Key Chapple has termed a "template" for his entire system. Three of the Yoga systems that Haribhadra investigates, and generally rejects, are Tantric. However, in his eightfold analysis of Yoga, which comprises over a third of the entire work, we see Haribhadra consciously adapting the eight-part practice into a Jain framework, linking it to the fourteen stages of purification and enlightenment of orthodox Jainism. This he does by identifying the inner restraints, the first component of the eight-part practice, with the first seven Jain stages of purification, with the remaining components, culminating in samadhi, tracking with the ascending trajectory of the Jain practitioner's progress toward the ultimate goal of omniscience and total inactivity.

We see a similar strategy being adopted by the twelfth-century Hemachandra, who became a highly influential minister to the western Indian king Kumarapala, a Hindu convert to Jainism. The author of another synthetic work, the *Yogashastra* ("Yoga Teaching"), Hemachandra follows Haribhadra in adapting the eight-part practice as both an organizing principle and a means to the Jain end of the realization of the Three Jewels of correct belief, knowledge, and conduct. This triad recalls the three yogas of the *Bhagavad Gita*, with which Hemachandra, as a former Hindu, would also have been fully acquainted. In order to realize the second jewel of knowledge, he argues, meditation is necessary, which presupposes the yogic postures. These are the subject of the final portion of Hemachandra's fourth chapter, which leads into an extended discussion of meditation and its prerequisites (including all of the other elements of the eight-part practice), which take up seven of the remaining eight chapters of the work. Hemachandra's twelfth and final chapter is based on another work, the eleventh- to twelfth-century "Non-Mental Yoga," which was, as we have noted, one of the earliest texts to address the distinction between Hatha and Raja Yoga. While the lion's share of Hemachandra's "Yoga Teaching" may be viewed as a Jain commentary on the *Yoga Sutra*, it should be noted that many of its concepts and meditative practices more † closely resemble Tantric Yoga traditions. While some of these traditions may be traced back to the Yogi Lords, who shared a number of cult centers with the Jains in western India, others likely originated in Kashmir, far to the north.

It was in Kashmir that Hindu Tantra reached its fullest flower in the extensive writings of the early eleventh-century philosopher and Tantra master Abhinavagupta. Often referred to as Kashmir Shaivism, the Tantric system Abhinavagupta's school elaborated offered three paths to self-divinization: ritual practice, gnosis, and Yoga. Broadly construed, the Tantric Yoga of this system involved an elaborate program of visionary meditation upon Tantric deities and mandalas. In this context Abhinavagupta and others from his † school explicitly referred, in several of their works, to various *Yoga Sutra* aphorisms concerning the supernatural powers and other topics. It is noteworthy that in at least one passage of his masterwork, the *Tantraloka* ("Elucidation of Tantra"), Abhinavagupta did so in order to dismiss Patanjali's eight-part practice as use- † less to the goals of the Tantric practitioner. Abhi- † navagupta quotes the *Yoga Sutra* more extensively in another of his works, the *Ishvarapratijnanavivritivimarshini* ("Critique of the Exposition of the Doctrine

† of Divine Recognition"). Significantly, he refers to Patanjali himself as Ananta, the divine "Lord of Serpents," an identification made earlier in the *Vishnudharmottara*, a Purana from Kashmir. Patanjali was particularly revered in Kashmir, not only because of this cachet of divinity, but also because the grammarian Patanjali mentions in his commentary that he had temporarily resided there. So it is that the *Yoga Sutra* is cited, for the most part favorably, by at least a dozen other Kashmirian authors from the same period.

Far to the south in Tamil Nadu, the same centuries saw Vaishnava theologians setting down the precepts of the orthodox Shrivaishnava school. Nathamuni, the tenth-century founder of the Shrivaishnava lineage, who will be discussed in another context in chapter 12, left no written teachings on the subject of Yoga. However, his disciple, Yadava Prakasha, who wrote 115 verses on the subject of Yoga in his *Yatidharmasamuccaya* ("Collection of Ascetic Practice"), cited nine aph-
† orisms from the *Yoga Sutra* and mentioned Patanjali by name. Third in this lineage was the illustrious Ramanuja, whose long life spanned 120 years of the elev-
† enth and twelfth centuries. The greatest of all Shrivaishnava theologians, he evoked the *Yoga Sutra*'s teachings in all three of his principal works, written on the subject of the Veda, Vedanta philosophy, and the *Bhagavad Gita* respectively. In contrast to the Advaita Vedanta doctrine of cosmic illusion, Ramanuja, an ex-
† ponent of the Qualified Nondualist school of Vedanta, maintained that the world was real, and that individ-

ual selves did exist. Although they could not be differentiated from their creator or cause (that is, a god with personal qualities such as Vishnu), these selves nonetheless did not possess God's powers of creation, omniscience, and so forth. By the same token, God, while "holographically" present in every individual self, could not be subject to the suffering or impurity that was the manifest lot of His creatures.

Ramanuja criticized several of the *Yoga Sutra*'s philosophical positions, including its metaphysical dualism and its goal of the isolation of Spirit from Nature; its view of the nature of the soul and of Ishvara; and the validity of direct yogic perception as a valid cognition and an unerring source of knowledge. He also rejected the *Yoga Sutra*'s goals, refusing to admit either the supernatural powers or samadhi. A staunch theist and fundamentalist with respect to scripture, Ramanuja's interest in the *Yoga Sutra* was practical: how to put its eight-part practice to use as a means to the supreme end of devotion to God. It was to this purpose that he prescribed the techniques of posture, breath control, and retraction of the senses as presented in the eight-part practice. He also prescribed meditation, but with an important caveat: it was not the technique of meditation that led to liberation, but rather its object, which for Ramanuja could only be God himself. No doubt unbeknownst to him, he was agreeing with the Muslim Alberuni, who had taken the same position over a century earlier. He was also agreeing with Vachaspati Mishra, but with an important distinction: for whereas Vishnu's outer form was, for the latter, a mere instrument to enhanced concentration, for Ramanuja, Vishnu was both the means and end of practice. Here he was simply reiterating the doctrines found in the Puranas and Smriti literature. By meditating on Vishnu, whom Ramanuja identified with the *Yoga Sutra*'s Ishvara, the practitioner would cultivate a personal relationship with Him, moving God to offer His grace and the practitioner's release

† from suffering existence. The sixteenth-century Vijnanabhikshu, who took much of his inspiration from Ramanuja, would identify Ishvara with the god

† Krishna. In the same period, Gaudiya Vaishnava theologians from Bengal would adapt the eight-part practice in a similar fashion, employing it as a technique leading to the soul's absorption into the object of meditation, Krishna. However, their source for the eight-part practice was more likely a Vaishnava Purana (such as the *Vishnu* or *Narada*) than the *Yoga Sutra* itself.

A most striking testimony to the prestige of the Yoga system in this period is a tenth-century work likely composed on the Indonesian island of Java. By the middle of the first millennium CE, Shaivism, the cult of the god Shiva whose mythology frequently casts him as a god of yoga, had emerged as the most important theistic system on the Indian subcontinent. (Shaivism still predominates in south India, whereas in the north, bhakti has, since the fifteenth century, evolved in a Vaishnava mode.) As we have seen, the most powerful and early sectarian proponents of the

Shaiva system, both institutionally and philosophically, were the Pashupatas. Already mentioned in the *Mahabharata*, they were responsible for the composition and reworking of several Puranas, and their institutional presence in South Asia is documented in nearly a hundred inscriptions that identify them as beneficiaries of land grants and other types of institutional support between the fifth and twelfth centuries.

During the same centuries, Hinduism came to be spread—through trade, conversion, and conquest— from India into much of Southeast Asia: a Javanese † translation of the *Mahabharata* has been dated to the eleventh century. And so it was that for several hundred years, kings from "Greater India" recruited Shaiva priests, many of them from the Pashupata order, to serve as their royal chaplains. During the same period, Shaiva priests and ascetics carried Pashupata teachings into rural areas where they fused with regional traditions to form new and original synergies. One of those † regional traditions, which emerged in the ninth century on the Indonesian islands of Java and Bali, revolved around a group called the Five Rishis ("Five Seers"), whose mythology portrayed them as both sons of Shiva and practitioners of Yoga responsible in part for the ordering of the universe. With a single ex- † ception, the names of these five figures were identical to those listed in the Shaiva Puranas and other early Indian traditions as the founding gurus of the Pashupata order: Kushika, Garga, Kurushya, and Maitri. In Indonesia, however, Lakulisha—the mythic founder of the Indian Pashupata lineage—was replaced by a figure named Patanjala. While it is tempting to see in the Rishi Patanjala's name a variant reading of Patanjali, this was not the case. Rather, the name was most likely derived from that of a south Indian cultural hero named Agastya, one of whose epithets was Pitanjala, "He Who Drank the Waters," a reference to a Puranic myth in which Agastya drank the entire ocean dry.

Regardless of the origin of his name, the mythic Indonesian Rishi Patanjala's prestige was so great that an important and unique tenth-century work written in Old Javanese came to be attributed to him. This work, titled *Dharma Patanjala* ("Sacred Teaching of Patanjala") has been preserved in a single fifteenth-century manuscript, which was discovered in western Java in the nineteenth century. In 2011, a critical translation and study of that manuscript was completed by the young Italian scholar Andrea Acri as his doctoral dissertation at Leiden University. I briefly summarize the remarkable content of that thesis here.

The "Sacred Teaching," which is cast as a dialogue between Shiva and his son Kumara, is, for the most part, a Pashupata treatise enshrining many elements of archaic Shaiva doctrine. The first two-thirds of its content, all presented along straightforward Pashupata lines, is devoted to such issues as epistemology, metaphysics, the nature of the soul, cosmology, embryology, physiology, theology, and doctrines of karma, rebirth, and liberation from rebirth. In the context of this last discussion the dialogue shades into the topic

of Yoga as the optimal path to release from suffering existence—and then, quite suddenly, becomes a paraphrase of much of the *Yoga Sutra*. Of the 161 verses of †
the *Yoga Sutra*'s first three chapters, all but thirty-seven are treated in the "Sacred Teaching"; however, the *Yoga Sutra*'s final chapter is entirely absent. Significantly, Patanjali is nowhere named as the source of this teaching on Yoga. Like the work translated by Alberuni in his "Book of the Indian Patanjali," the version of the *Yoga Sutra* paraphrased into Old Javanese in the "Sacred Teaching" diverges on several points from Patanjali's work as it was known to its classical Indian commentators. This has led scholars to surmise †
that like Alberuni, the Javanese author of the "Sacred Teaching" was working from an earlier and now lost version of the *Yoga Sutra*. Some have concluded that independent of the evidence found in these two foreign translations, the entire fourth chapter of the *Yoga Sutra* was a late addition. I will return to this matter in the final chapter of this book.

The Yoga of the Pashupata and later Shaiva systems was not the same as that espoused in the *Yoga Sutra*, and the early Shaiva scriptures took great pains to make this distinction. Rather than the isolation of Spirit from Nature, the Pashupatas defined the goal of †
Yoga as the union or contact of the individual soul with God, by virtue of which the human yogi could come to manifest the attributes—that is, the eight supernatural powers—of Shiva himself (without actually becoming God or losing himself in God). While

this was the orthodox Shaiva position, later Shaiva treatments of Yoga, as found in the Puranas as well as the Shaiva scriptures known as the Agamas and Tantras, came to diverge from those of the original *Pashupata Sutras* on a number of points. Many of these divergences reflected an attempt to synthesize Shaiva Yoga with elements of the eight-part practice. However, as was the case with the Puranic and other systems, the sole effective object of Shaiva meditation remained the god Shiva himself.

Such attempts at synthesis are documented not only in the Shaiva Puranas but also in many of the post-ninth-century Shaiva Agamas and Tantras, as well as in several Agamic and Tantric commentaries. Regardless of whether the *Yoga Sutra* was their source, this adaptation of the eight-part practice was no small thing, because it supplanted the earlier Pashupata sequence, which had been limited to six parts. This sequence, first attested in the *Maitri Upanishad*, usually comprised breath control, retraction of the senses, meditation, fixation, and pure contemplation, with philosophical reflection (tarka) replacing posture (asana). Breaking ranks with all other Old Javanese texts (and possibly all earlier Shaiva works from India), the "Sacred Teaching" not only presented the *Yoga Sutra*'s eight-part practice in its entirety, but also appropriated the first three chapters of *Yoga Sutra* in such a way as to fit Patanjali's Yoga system into an archaic Shaiva framework. Here, the *Yoga Sutra* aphorisms were presented in their original sequence, but they were reshaped into a commentary that, like that of Alberuni's work, was cast in a dialogue format, in this case between Shiva and his divine son Kumara.

While orthodox Shaiva doctrine is Dualist (one can become like Shiva, but never become merged into Shiva, or become Shiva himself), several Tantric schools (including that of Abhinavagupta) were Nondualist. In the case of the "Sacred Teaching," both positions are entertained. Central to its reworking of the *Yoga Sutra* is its identification of Patanjali's Ishvara †
with Shiva himself, who teaches Kumara that He lives from one cosmic cycle to the next by manifesting His divine powers in a yogi whose concentration is pure. In fact, earlier Pashupata works had already identified †
Rudra with the transcendent twenty-sixth principle, paralleling trends found in the *Mahabharata* and other works, as mentioned in chapter 2. However, the †
pure contemplation of the realized yogi is equated here not with the samadhi of the *Yoga Sutra*, but rather with the Pashupata definition of Yoga. It is a level of omniscience and omnipotence equal to that of God himself—with the important difference being that while this is God's innate and eternal nature, for the yogi it can only be acquired at the end of many lives of practice. Even so, the "Sacred Teaching" identifies the †
ultimate goal of the *Yoga Sutra*'s eight-part practice as union with Shiva and the attainment of His supernatural powers, reflecting the normative devotional Hindu reading of yoga as "union."

Elsewhere, the "Sacred Teaching" introduces the *Yoga Sutra*'s discussion of the postures by prescribing a
† set of purifying mantras unique to Pashupata tradi-
† tions. Certain elements of its account of the supernatural powers of the yogi draw on Shaiva and Tantric traditions unknown to either Patanjali or Vyasa. One of these, the fantasy of every seminary student, is the power of fully knowing the sacred scriptures without having to read them first: this is not found in the *Yoga Sutra*, but is commonly listed in Puranic presentations
† of the Yoga system. Most interesting is its innovative adaptation of *Yoga Sutra* 3.38, which deals with the ability of a realized yogi to enter into the bodies of other creatures. Unlike the classical commentaries, our Javanese text links this power to the classic form of Tantric initiation in which a Tantric guru fuses his breath channels together with those of his pupil, after which he enters his body to initiate him from within.

Ishvara

For most of the nineteenth century following Colebrooke's "discovery" of the *Yoga Sutra*, Patanjali's work was, for the most part, instrumentalized by various and sundry philosophers, mystics, and reformers for their own ulterior motives. Hegel appropriated selected portions of Colebrooke's account of the work to knock together the heads of the brothers Schlegel. Madame Blavatsky and W. Q. Judge promulgated their fuzzy notions of Yoga philosophy mainly for purposes of self-promotion. Swami Vivekananda used his teachings on "Raja Yoga" to raise funds and to serve as a platform for his gospel of Indian exceptionalism and the scientific foundations of ancient Hindu thought. As we have seen, none of these individuals, with the exception of Vivekananda, was capable of reading the *Yoga Sutra* or its original authoritative commentaries in the original Sanskrit. Yet even with his proficiency in that ancient language, Vivekananda gave little heed to the work's commentarial tradition in composing his own commentary. Like the Theosophists, he trusted his own powers of intuition and reason to gain an immediate, unmediated understanding of a fourth-century text, relegating the intervening history of *Yoga Sutra* commentary by some of India's greatest minds to the dustbin of history.

In sharp distinction to this cavalier approach, critical scholars, both Indian and Western, working in the wake of Colebrooke and the British Orientalists, have taken the text and its commentarial traditions as the principal objects of their investigation. For much of the nineteenth century following Colebrooke's 1823 essay, critical scholarship on the *Yoga Sutra* was limited to the publication of workable editions of the text and its principal commentaries. These included the Ballantyne–Shastri Deva (1852/1885) and Mitra (1883) editions and translations of the *Yoga Sutra* with Bhoja's "Royal Sun" commentary; Ramakrishna Shastri and Keshava Shastri's poorly edited 1884 edition of the *Yoga Sutra* with Vijnanabhikshu's "Explanation of Yoga"; Jibananda Vidyasagara's 1874 edition with Vachaspati Mishra's "Expert Guide to the True Principles" (a superior edition of the same was published by Rajaram Shastri Bodas in 1890); Ganganath Jha's 1894 edition and translation of Vijnanabhikshu's "Short Statement"; and a handful of other editions of the text and various commentaries.

Shortly after the publication of these various editions, a series of new studies began to appear that gradually fleshed out the bare bones of Colebrooke's original essay, as scholars sought to hone in on the originality, specificity, and possible sources of Patanjali's teaching. After Mitra, the most important among these was Friedrich Max Müller's *Six Systems*, published in 1899. The scion of a German Romantic family of some renown, Max Müller was an Orientalist in the finest sense of the term, combining careful philological analysis with a rigorous historical and critical approach to the study of religion. Trained in Berlin and Paris, Max Müller gravitated to Oxford University in 1851, where he remained until his death in 1900. His scholarly output was staggering, even if not all of his theories—of a universal "solar mythology," for example—have stood the test of time. An important pivot between the India of the Romantic imagination and the India of critical scholarship, he continues to be renowned in modern-day India by his sobriquet Moksh Mula, a play on words that etymologizes his name as "Root of Liberation" in Sanskrit and other Indo-Aryan languages.

Max Müller was a pivotal figure for a number of reasons. Like Vivekananda, he was attracted to the Brahmo Samaj, and through it to Ramakrishna, about whom he wrote a book and several essays. Vivekananda †
noted this in an article, published in 1896 after a visit to Max Müller at Oxford, in which he lauded him as "a Vedantist of Vedantists [who] has . . . caught the real soul of the melody of the Vedanta . . . the one light that lightens the sects and creeds of the world, the Vedanta, the one principle of which all religions are only appli-

cations."[1] For his part, Max Müller appears to be addressing Vivekananda, the Brahmo Samaj, and other proponents of Neo-Vedanta in the preface to his *Six Systems*, where he despairs at the disappearance of traditional philosophical instruction in India and cautions against false prophets:

† But though we may regret that the ancient method of philosophical study is dying out in India, we should welcome all the more a new class of native students who, after studying the history of European philosophy, have devoted themselves to the honorable task of making their own national philosophy better known to the world at large. I hope that my book may prove useful to them by showing them in what direction they may best assist us in our attempts to secure a place to thinkers such as Kapila and Badarayana by the side of the leading philosophers of Greece, Rome, Germany, France, Italy, and England. In some cases the enthusiasm of native students may seem to have carried them too far, and a mixing up of philosophical with religious and theosophic propaganda, inevitable as it is said to be in India, is always dangerous.[2]

The overview of Indian philosophy that Max Müller presents in his *Six Systems* is possessed of a clarity that has eluded many who have followed. His discussions of the various schools, lucid and compelling in and of themselves, are greatly enhanced by his ability to recreate the cultural and philosophical contexts within

which the schools developed and interacted. Like the †
classical commentators, as well as Colebrooke and
other critical scholars before him, Max Müller identifies the *Yoga Sutra*'s eight-part practice and its focus on
Ishvara as the principal differentiates between Yoga
and Samkhya. He also follows Colebrooke in his tepid
appreciation of the specificity of Yoga philosophy with
respect to Samkhya, comparing it to the popery of the
Catholic Church (like nearly all of his Oxford colleagues, Max Müller was a Protestant):

> The real relation of the soul to the body and of the †
> senses to the soul is still as great a mystery to us as it
> was to the ancient Yogins of India, and their expe-
> riences, if only honestly related, deserve certainly
> the same careful attention as the stigmata of
> Roman Catholic saints. They may be or they may
> not be true, but there is no reason why they should
> be treated as a priori untrue. From this point of
> view it seems to me that the Yoga-philosophy de-
> serves some attention on the part of philosophers,
> more particularly of the physical school of psychol-
> ogists, and I did not feel justified therefore in pass-
> ing over this system altogether, though it may be
> quite true that, after we have once understood the
> position of the Samkhya-philosophy towards the
> great problem of the world, we shall not glean
> many new metaphysical or psychological ideas
> from a study of the Yoga.[3]

Much of Max Müller's discussion of the *Yoga Sutra* is devoted to the question of the nature and identity of Ishvara. As we have already seen, this was clearly a major point of contention among the classical commentators, as evidenced by the fact that they, as a group, devoted more space to this matter than to any other topic in the entire work. In short, their debate revolved around the question of whether the first letter of the word Ishvara was an uppercase or a lowercase *i*. We have already surveyed a number of opinions, by figures ranging from the anonymous authors of the Puranas to Vedanta theologians like Shankara, Ramanuja, and Vijnanabhikshu to such non-Indian interpreters as Alberuni, Weber, and Monier-Williams.

† In Patanjali's work, Ishvara is the subject of six sutras, which indicate that a practitioner may stop the fluctuations of his mind through "commitment to Ish-
† vara." The same practice is also listed as one of the three components of practical yoga (kriya yoga) and as one of the outer observances (niyamas) of the eight-part practice.

The Sanskrit word I have translated here as "commitment" is pranidhana, which critical scholars have variously read as "dedication," "profound longing,"
† "contemplation," and even "meditation." In the context of Mahayana Buddhism, the term denotes the "vow" a future bodhisattva takes to save all sentient beings from suffering existence. However, as I have already noted, many commentators and no small num-

ber of scholars have preferred to read pranidhana as "devotion," and to construe Ishvara as a transcendent twenty-sixth principle and one of the gods of the new Hindu theism. In support of this reading, some have noted Vyasa's interpretation of pranidhana as prasada, †
a word that commonly means the saving "grace" of an all-powerful creator God. This position appears to have been shared by Vachaspati Mishra, who implies that the practice of Yoga, including devotion to God, leads to release. The modern-day yoga guru Swami †
Venkatesananda takes matters a step further, translating the term as "surrender," arguing that it alone is sufficient for the realization of the isolation of Spirit from Matter. In this case, Yoga practice simply becomes an alternate form of Hindu devotion *pace* the Puranas in which surrendering to God is reciprocated by His grace and the promise of salvation.

However, as Arion Roşu and Olivier Lacombe †
have notably argued, prasada would have been understood by Patanjali and his contemporaries as "serenity," or a "state of trans-luminous peace," and ishvara-pranidhana as "the serenity one acquires through the help of a Master of Yoga."[4] Commitment to such a Master would in no way have implied devotion to a deity of any sort. Indeed, in the centuries prior to the *Yoga Sutra*'s time, the word "ishvara" had never de-†
noted a god, but was rather applied to a human lord or king: this was the meaning adduced by Patanjali the grammarian in his "Great Commentary." Then, in the centuries around the time of our work, its usage was

expanded and came to be employed as an epithet or descriptor of this or that god. Nonetheless, in his commentary on *Yoga Sutra* 1.25, Vyasa clearly intends ishvara in the earlier sense of the word, identifying Kapila, the legendary founder of Samkhya philosophy, as
† an exemplary ishvara. Barbara Stoler Miller's interpretation of this sutra respects that of Vyasa: "the Lord [Master of Yoga] is not a creator god who grants grace; rather, he is a representation of the omniscient spirit as the archetypal yogi."[5] In this context, pranidhana means "commitment to the discipline represented by the Lord of Yoga." This, as Max Müller explained over a hundred years ago, was undoubtedly Patanjali's understanding of the term:

† The Isvara, with the Yogins, was originally no more than one of the many souls, or rather Selves or Purusas, but one that has never been associated or implicated in metempsychosis, supreme in every sense, yet of the same kind as all other Purusas. The idea of other Purusas obtaining union with him could therefore never have entered Patanjali's head.[6]

Many modern-day scholar-practitioners take issue with this reading, following the leads of Ramanuja, Vijnanabhikshu, and other proponents of a theistic
† reading of the term. A case in point is Edwin Bryant, who, in his recent splendid commentary on the *Yoga Sutra*, notes that Vijnanabhikshu considered ishvara-pranidhana to refer to the practice of devotion to

Krishna, the Lord of the *Bhagavad Gita*. Bryant clearly aligns himself with this interpretation of the term, reading ishvara-pranidhana as submission to a personal god and asserting that most yogis over the past two millennia have been associated with devotional sects. It should be noted here that the *Bhagavad Gita* and other Vaishnava scriptures frequently identified Krishna as the "supreme Purusha" (purushottama) and maintained that He creates, maintains, and destroys the worlds out of his love for His creatures. Furthermore, the *Gita* also referred to Krishna as a Master of †
Yoga, a yogeshvara (a compound composed of yoga + ishvara). In it, Krishna's characterization of the ideal †
yogi as a person who "sees me in everything and sees everything in me" could be read as a rewording of Patanjali's ishvara-pranidhana.

Now, if, as Bryant implies, Patanjali was a practitioner of Yoga and a devotee of a personal god like Krishna, he may well have been thinking of "devotion to God" when he employed the term ishvara-pranidhana. This being said, we cannot know whether or to what extent Patanjali or Vyasa were aware of the *Bhagavad Gita* and its doctrines. While our best evidence indicates that the *Yoga Sutra* was compiled at about the same time as the *Bhagavad Gita*, neither work makes any explicit reference to the other. Of course, both likely drew on oral traditions that circulated, perhaps in the same circles, for some time (decades? centuries?) before they were committed to writing, and it was precisely in the first centuries of the

Common Era that oral traditions began to be committed to writing in South Asia. In the *Mahabharata*'s twelfth book, which was likely compiled within a century or two of both of these works, we encounter the term ishvara yet again, but this time in the plural. Here, ishvaras are yogis who, by virtue of their power of yoga are "masters" capable of simultaneously entering into the bodies of multiple creatures—gods, sages, and great beings—in much the same way as the Master of Yoga Krishna is seen doing in the *Bhagavad Gita*. Centuries later, the *Linga Purana* and several Tantric works would elevate such Masters of Yoga to the level of deities able to function as savior figures to their disciples, through initiation and teaching. Subverting all of these interpretations, however, is the reading suggested by Arthur Berriedale Keith, who argued that Patanjali's definition of Ishvara as "the one in which the seed of omniscience reaches the highest degree"[7] was a direct reference to concepts found in Mahayana and Yogacara Buddhism! In the light of these conflicting interpretations, it is unlikely that there will ever be a final word on what Patanjali meant by ishvara-pranidhana.

Journeys East, Journeys West
The *Yoga Sutra* in the Early Twentieth Century

The decades that followed Vivekananda's triumphal mission to the West were the stage for what has been   †
termed India's "Yoga Renaissance." For the most part, this new flowering of yoga took place on Indian soil, with only two of its leading figures actually following Vivekananda to the West. The most illustrious of these was Paramahansa Yogananada, who settled in the United States in 1920, teaching and lecturing there for decades before his highly inspirational *Autobiography of a Yogi* was published in 1946, six years prior to his death. While he called his particular synthesis Kriya Yoga, the term used for "practical yoga" in *Yoga Sutra* 2.1–27, Patanjali's work is conspicuously absent from his writings. Rather, the *Autobiography* emphasizes the scientific foundations of yoga practice, the links between Indian and Christian spirituality, and the miraculous supernatural powers of India's yogis. Another yoga master who briefly traveled to the United States in the same period was Shri Yogendra,

who sought to debunk the teachings of such self-proclaimed practitioners of Tantric Yoga as Aleistair Crowley and Pierre Bernard. However, the Yoga Institutes he founded during the years he remained in the New York area were, for all intensive purposes, medical clinics.

Why other members of that first generation of post-Vivekanandan yoga specialists did not follow in the Swami's footsteps had much to do with American xenophobia. A series of restrictive immigration acts passed between 1917 and 1929 barred nearly all Asians from so much as entering the country. It was not until 1965, when that act was amended and Asian immigration quotas lifted, that Indian gurus were allowed to return to the United States—just in time for the cultural revolution that was sweeping the country. During the intervening half-century, most Americans seeking instruction in yoga and the *Yoga Sutra* from Indian gurus and scholars had to travel to India to do so. Of course, the Vedanta and Theosophical Society's western beachheads continued to retail Indian wisdom in major urban centers, and Yoga scholars in India and the West could communicate through publications and correspondence. In addition, some Indian yoga gurus, as imperial subjects, did journey to Great Britain. For the most part, however, modern Indian and Western interpretations and appropriations of the *Yoga Sutra* followed separate tracks, with India lagging behind the West for several decades.

During the first decades of the twentieth century, the *Yoga Sutra* was widely ignored in India; the founding fathers of the Yoga Renaissance barely mention the work. One of these was the Bengali freedom fighter Aurobindo Ghosh, better known as Shri Aurobindo, who was imprisoned by the British for his revolutionary activities in 1908. After his release in 1909, he fled British India for the French enclave of Pondicherry on India's southeastern coast, where he gave up his political activities for the inner, spiritual life. Aurobindo had had a number of transformative mystical experiences during his year of incarceration, which led to the development of his own system of Yoga. That system, detailed in his 1914–21 *Synthesis of Yoga* relied heavily on the *Bhagavad Gita* while ignoring the *Yoga Sutra*. Already in 1912, Aurobindo was certain of the distinctiveness of his own path, noting that his was "not the conventional method of Patanjali," but "the natural method" he had "stumbled upon in his meditations."[1] Looking back on those breakthroughs, he would attribute his inspiration to Vivekananda: "I began my Yoga in 1904. My Sadhana [practice] was not founded upon books but upon personal experience that crowded on me from within. . . . It is a fact that I was hearing constantly the voice of Vivekananda speaking to me for a fortnight in the Jail."[2] As Peter Heehs has observed, Aurobindo's synthesis was closer to that of Tantric Yoga, whose goal was the transformation of the world and life (shakti) as opposed to the isolation of Spirit from Nature. A crucial element of Aurobindo's Yoga, concerning the passage from mind to "supermind," was influenced by Nietzsche's theory of the "super-man," but was also redolent of the evolutionist theories of Vivekananda and the Theosophists. Although he does not refer to it directly in his *Synthesis of Yoga*, Aurobindo does appear to have taken the *Yoga Sutra*'s aphorisms on the supernatural powers (siddhis) as his inspiration for the final chapters of his unfinished work.

Embracing Vivekananda's Neo-Vedanta teachings on Yoga as an ancient Indian science, two of Aurobindo's contemporaries established yoga research centers in western India: these were Shri Yogendra and Swami Kuvalayananda, the two yoga gurus most responsible for the early "medicalization" of yoga in India. Their innovations lay the foundation for the principal tenet of modern postural yoga practice, that is, that yoga is primarily a set of techniques for realizing and maintaining good health. Both of these figures claimed Madhavdas, a former civil servant who had renounced the world to practice yoga in the Himalayas in the late nineteenth century, as their teacher. In spite of Madhavdas's allegiance to Vivekananda's teachings, however, neither of his disciples saw fit to showcase the *Yoga Sutra* in their respective syntheses.

Shri Yogendra founded his Yoga Institute in Mumbai in 1918, to which he returned and remained following four years of clinical practice in New York between 1919 and 1923. In 1924 Kuvalayananda established his Kaivalyadhama Yoga Ashram about thirty miles to the southeast, at Lonavla in the state of Maharashtra. The yoga that both promulgated was entirely devoted to placing yoga physiology in the service of general health and physical fitness, which for Kuvalayananda meant going back to the sources—in his case the "Little Lamp" and other Hatha Yoga works—to recover the yogic science of the ancients. Kuvalayananda did, however, write a series of studies of Patanjali's sutras on † breath control and meditation, which appeared in the 1956 and 1957 issues of *Yoga Mimamsa*, the Kaivalyadhama Yoga Ashram's scientific yoga journal.

Another giant of the Indian Yoga Renaissance was Swami Sivananda. The scion of an illustrious south Indian priestly lineage turned Western medical doctor, he had given up his practice in Malaysia to settle in Rishikesh, in the Himalayan foothills, in 1920. There he established a yoga ashram that would become the headquarters for his Divine Life Society, which he founded in 1936. In 1935, he wrote *The Science of* † *Pranayama*, one of the first of his hundreds of publications that followed Vivekananda's lead by bringing together the language of science, physiology, and health to explain "liberation" in terms of prana. Sivananda's teachings and writings differed from those of Vivekananda on two major points. One of these was his emphasis on celibacy and semen retention as essential to Indian masculinity; the other was a formulation of Raja Yoga that, fusing Hatha Yoga and Vedanta, en- † tirely bypassed the teachings of the *Yoga Sutra*.

That none of these giants of India's early twentieth-century Yoga Renaissance chose to include the *Yoga*

Sutra in their innovative adaptations (or reinventions) of yoga is yet another indication of the fact that India generally remained a "Yoga desert" well beyond the nineteenth-century publication of Sanskrit and English editions of the *Yoga Sutra*. Vivekananda's *Raja Yoga* was, in many respects, a foreign work, written in the West by a western-educated Indian for a Western readership. It would not be until the publication of works in regional languages by Hariharananda Aranya and Tirumalai Krishnamacharya that Indian masters would integrate the *Yoga Sutra* into works targeting an Indian readership. As we will see, however, in the case of Krishnamacharya, the *Yoga Sutra* was far less important to the master himself than it has been for two of his most illustrious disciples, who, in their respective struggles to claim the mantle of their teacher's legacy, have since the 1990s made him out to be the greatest *Yoga Sutra* connoisseur of the modern era.

† One of the most illustrious foreign guests in the early days of Sivananda's Rishikesh ashram was Mircea Eliade, the Romanian scholar who would become the mid-twentieth century's premier specialist of both yoga and Yoga philosophy. On the rebound from a disastrous romance with the daughter of his Bengali mentor, the philosopher Surendranath Dasgupta, Eliade had, in the fall of 1930, fled what he called "historical India" for the "eternal India" of Sivananda's Himalayan ashram. During his six months there, he lived the life of a renouncer, wearing the ocher robes of a yogi, begging his food with a brass bowl, bathing in the

churning snow-fed waters of the holy river, and most importantly for his research, conversing with the Swami and his fellow hermits on the subjects of philosophy and Sanskrit. At the time of Eliade's departure, Sivananda predicted that he would become the "next Vivekananda," spreading the message of yoga and Vedanta throughout the West. Eliade demurred, † remarking that he found Vivekananda's writings to be superficial.

Yoga: Immortality and Freedom, Eliade's most important work on Yoga—and, arguably the most significant of his hundreds of publications on the history of world religions—first appeared in French in 1954. Some twenty years in the making, it slowly evolved out of the doctoral dissertation he had submitted to the University of Bucharest in 1933 under the title "The Psychology of Indian Meditation." As Eliade noted in † his 1954 foreword, Patanjali's system was not his major concern. Rather, his was an effort to distinguish Yoga philosophy from what it was not (Tantra, devotional Hinduism, Hatha Yoga) and to situate it in its broader South Asian contexts. However, we also see him elaborating one of the pervasive themes of his broader oeuvre: that archaic systems of thought—in this case India's Yoga traditions—could, if recovered by modern man, free humanity from its existential condition, what Eliade called the "terror of history."

For Eliade, classical Yoga was a "living fossil, a mo- † dality of archaic spirituality that has survived nowhere else."[3] Integral to that spirituality was an ancient form of psychoanalysis and a thoroughgoing investigation into the role of the subconscious. This theme, which we see in the title of Eliade's 1933 dissertation, is one that he returned to repeatedly in his writing on Yoga. Yoga was a path of self-analysis, but one whose goals transcended those of psychoanalysis inasmuch as it led not only to an understanding of the contents of the unconscious mind but also to mastery over them, and ultimately to their destruction.

This was samadhi. Eliade was not alone in this reading of Patanjali, a fact he acknowledged in his earliest

† French-language publication on Yoga. On the first page of this 1936 work, he cited two scholars: his Indian mentor Dasgupta and the German Yoga scholar

† Jakob Wilhelm Hauer. In 1932, Hauer had published a book titled *Der Yoga als Heilweg* ("Yoga as a Path to Salvation") in which he argued for the psychoanalytic value of Patanjali's system, a theme he would greatly expand upon in a revised version of the book,

† written in 1958. In the latter work, Hauer also shows his clear indebtedness to the ideas of Carl Gustav Jung, with whom he frequently met and collaborated in the 1930s. Eliade also interacted with Jung, collaborating with him in 1951 on the seminal Eranos Jahrbuch titled *Mensch und Zeit* ("Man and Time"). For

† much of the 1920s and 1930s, Jung himself had been strongly influenced by Patanjali's "Yoga psychology," but had abandoned it for reasons nearly identical to those marshaled by Hegel about a century earlier. In the end, Jung had rejected Patanjali's system, maintain-

ing that it collapsed psychology into philosophy and was grounded in broad metaphysical concepts that had little relation to empirical facts or psychological experience. Furthermore, because the East had not yet reached the level of self-awareness achieved in Western scientific thought, it was not possessed of a psychology in the Western sense of the word: it was, rather, "pre-psychological." Furthermore, Jung could not reconcile his view of the role of the ego in mystical experience with Patanjali's description of samadhi, which required the complete negation of the ego.

Unlike the Swiss Jung, the German Hauer and the Romanian Eliade perceived another dimension to Yoga, which resonated with their adherence to the causes of National Socialism and Fascism. For Eliade, †
his scholarship on Yoga in particular had a political significance, which he closely linked to the rise of the Iron Guard, the nationalist and anti-Semitic movement he had joined in 1937. For Hauer, who was in- †
ducted into the SS by Heinrich Himmler in 1933, yoga was a quintessentially Aryan phenomenon, an ancient Indo-Germanic tradition that glorified the heroic death of both the warrior and the yogi. His linking of the two worlds is made explicit in the final paragraph of his 1932 work (which he also reprinted in full in his 1958 revised edition). Here, after praising Vijnana-bhikshu for his engaging presentation of the entire Yoga system, he concluded his work by offering a sort †
of millenarian vision of the reforging, through Vive-kananda's transmission of the *Yoga Sutra* to the West,

of the ancient bond between two the great strands of the Indo-Germanic *Geist*.

Eliade was the first leading Western scholar of Yoga to combine some personal experience of yoga with formal academic training. As we have noted, since the time of Madame Blavatsky, a clear line has generally separated persons seeking practical knowledge of yoga from others seeking historical and theoretical knowledge of the *Yoga Sutra* and Yoga philosophy. A classic example of the gulf separating the two camps are the reviews received by James Haughton Woods's 1914 translation of the *Yoga Sutra* with the commentaries of Vyasa and Vachaspati Mishra. A highly peripatetic scholar, Woods had spent two decades preparing his translation, studying with the greatest luminaries of the time at Harvard, Oxford, Cambridge, Bonn, Berlin, Varanasi, Srinagar, and Pune. Now a full century after its original publication, Woods's translation continues to receive praise from critical scholars as a model of technical precision and rigor. But poetry it is not.

† By way of example, his translation of *Yoga Sutra* 4.9 reads as follows: "There is an uninterrupted [causal] relation [of subconscious impressions], although remote in species and point-of-space and movement-of-time, by reason of the correspondence between memory and subliminal-impressions."

While for many scholars Woods's translation is a gold standard to be emulated—as many have done in

† subsequent translations—mere mortals, as one of his early scholarly reviewers noted, may find his English to

be as impenetrable as the original Sanskrit. This appears to have been the case for one of Woods's most critical readers, a celebrated poet who collaborated with a traditional Indian guru on a quite different translation of Patanjali's text. This was William Butler Yeats, who toward the end of his life was a disciple of an Indian holy man named Shri Purohit Swami. The two collaborated on translations of several works of Indian spirituality, including the *Yoga Sutra*, and Shri Purohit Swami's readings of Patanjali's work come through in several of Yeats's essays.

Like nearly all of his contemporaries, Shri Purohit Swami read the *Yoga Sutra* through the lens of Vedanta, identifying Yoga as union with God. Two decades later, Swami Prabhavananda, founder of the Vedanta Society of Southern California, would, together with his illustrious understudy Christopher Isherwood, define Yoga in the same way, further asserting that "yoga, prior to Patanjali, was originally grounded in Vedanta philosophy."[4] So too, Krishnamacharya and his principal disciples have equated Yoga with the union of the individual self with the cosmic or transcendent Self. These and the majority of twentieth- and twenty-first-century yoga gurus who have written "commentaries" on the *Yoga Sutra* combine these common elements of pandit lore with folksy stories about holy men they have known, which are intended to communicate the subtleties of Yoga philosophy in ways that their "children" can understand.

It is Yeats's own voice, however, that one clearly hears in his 1937 introduction to Shri Purohit Swami's translation of the *Yoga Sutra*. His essay opens with a reference to "a famous poet and student of Samskrit [*sic*], who used it as a dictionary."[5] Here, he was refer-
† ring to none other than T. S. Eliot, who had studied Sanskrit under Woods at Harvard during the 1911/12
† academic year, at a time when Patanjali's work was his guide to life as well as the inspiration for his theoretical approach to the psychology of reading and writing. It may also have inspired him to write his most ac-
† claimed work of poetry. As his biographer Cleo Kearns has suggested, the metaphor of root and rebirth in the opening verses of Eliot's *The Waste Land* is best comprehended when read through the lens of Patanjali's analysis of subliminal impressions and the seeds of karma from past lives:

> April is the cruelest month, breeding
> Lilacs out of the dead land, mixing
> Memory and desire, stirring
> Dull roots with spring rain.

While Woods's translation and interpretation of the *Yoga Sutra* played a formative role in Eliot's development as a poet, for Yeats his prose style left much to be desired.

† Some years ago I bought *The Yoga-System of Patanjali*, translated and edited by James Horton [*sic*]

Woods and published by the Harvard Press. It is the standard edition, final, impeccable in scholastic eyes.... Certainly before the Ajanta Caves were painted ... naked ascetics had put what they believed an ancient wisdom into short aphorisms for their pupils to get by heart and put into practice. I come in my turn, no grammarian, but a man engaged in that endless research into life, death, God, that is every man's revery. I want to hear the talk of those naked men, and I am certain they never said "The subliminal impression produced this (super reflective balanced state)" nor talked of "predicate relations."[6]

While both Yeats and Eliot were members of the Theosophical Society, Eliade and Jung were openly critical of the group. Their view was shared by another member of the European literati, the Hungarian Arthur Koestler, who in 1942 inveighed against "the hacks of Yogi-journalese" and "crank philosophers who dispense a minimum of information about breathing-technique wrapped in a maximum of obscurantist bombast."[7] In 1959, Koestler was able to combine a lecture tour to India and Japan with his own ethnographic and literary study of India's Yoga traditions. The result was his 1960 book, *The Lotus and the Robot*, in which he addressed the *Yoga Sutra*'s discussion of the supernatural powers. Here, he rightly argued, contra the bowdlerized readings of the Theosophists Wood and Judge, that Patanjali had identified the power to enter into another body, omnipotence, and levitation as legitimate rewards for persons who had mastered the higher forms of contemplation. He also noted that this was the general consensus among the Indian practitioners of yoga he had interviewed.

Koestler was the last member of the Western literati to pay serious heed to the *Yoga Sutra*. After 1965—the year in which relaxed immigration policies opened the way for Indian gurus to flow into the United States just as the counterculture movement was gaining momentum in the West—that torch would be taken up again by members of the emergent yoga subculture. The first seeds of that subculture had already been planted in 1952, when the New York–born violinist Yehudi Menuhin first began practicing yoga under the tutelage of B.K.S. Iyengar.

It was in 1967 however, that yoga truly burst into the collective Western consciousness, when the Beatles met and subsequently introduced Maharishi Mahesh Yogi and his program of Transcendental Meditation

† (TM) to the world. The Maharishi made the cover of *Time* magazine in 1975, but in the same year, the movement stalled, with monthly teacher training enrollments dropping by 90 percent in the two years that followed. It was then, in 1977, that a new TM product called the TM-Sidhi program was introduced. Ostensibly based on the third chapter of the *Yoga Sutra*, this was nothing less than training in supernatural powers,

† with an emphasis on levitation, or "yogic flying." This program, which the Maharishi University of Manage-

ment website indicates "was brought to light by Maharishi from the *Yoga Sutras* of Patanjali," involves mentally repeating the "flying sutra" or one of the other †
sutras on the supernatural powers (siddhis).[8] In the case of yogic flying, practitioners begin by hopping on firm foam mattresses in the cross-legged posture. Eventually, they hover, and finally they fly. Neither this power, nor the many other benefits claimed by the program (increases in "brain wave coherence," reduced rates of crime, sickness and accidents, world peace) have ever been substantiated.

The Strange Case of
T. M. Krishnamacharya

No person on the planet has had a greater impact on contemporary yoga practice than Tirumalai Krishnamacharya. The guru of B.K.S. Iyengar, K. Pattabhi Jois, and T.K.V. Desikachar, Krishnamacharya was the innovator of many if not most of the postures and sequences now taught in yoga centers and studios around the world. Intellectual brilliance, creativity, yogic powers, Sanskrit scholarship, philosophical acumen, pedagogical skills, healing gifts, and spirituality: all of these qualities and achievements have contributed to giving this spare, wiry individual larger than life dimensions. Hundreds of photographs of both the teacher himself and his illustrious pupils and protégés are proof positive of his virtuoso command of postural yoga. With respect to Yoga philosophy, however, the picture is less clear. Nearly all that we know of Krishnamacharya's philosophical background has come down to us through the filter of five authorized biographical notices—one is tempted to say hagiographies—four of which were written by his son and disciple T.K.V. Desikachar and his grandson Kausthub Desikachar, in 1982, 1997, 1998, and 2005. The picture that emerges from these books is one of a great intellect combined with superhuman powers of body, vision, and insight, and an all-consuming thirst for yogic knowledge—which, as his biographers reiterate ad infinitum, was grounded in an unrivaled mastery of the philosophy of the *Yoga Sutra*.

As his biographers note, the salient facts of Krishnamacharya's life are known through eleven pages of autobiographical notes written by him near the end of his life, as well as from their own accounts of his reminiscences and teachings to them. It is therefore curious that these facts have changed with each new biography: what one in fact sees in these books is a process of legacy building, of transforming an innovator of postural yoga into a "universal man" of Yoga. According to these family traditions, Krishnamacharya became an accomplished master of Yoga through his "genealogical bloodline" and three types of training: direct revelation, a conventional academic education, and discipleship under a trans-Himalayan Yoga master. †

The scion of an illustrious family of brahmin intellectuals, the young Krishnamacharya received a traditional religious education at the brahmin college of Parakala in Mysore, the greatest center of Shrivaishnava learning in all of south India, where his grandfather was the abbot. Prior even to his formal schooling at Parakala, Krishnamacharya had been initiated into †

Yoga at age five when his father began to teach him aphorisms from Patanjali's *Yoga Sutra*. His father had also revealed to him that he was directly descended from the revered tenth-century yogi Nathamuni, the founder of the Shrivaishnava school. At sixteen, the young Krishnamacharya journeyed alone to Nathamuni's birthplace. There he fell into a trance state in which he received the entire teaching of a lost Yoga work, the *Yoga Rahasya* ("Secret Teaching on Yoga"), from Nathamuni himself. This was the beginning of his Yoga quest. In the words of his grandson Kausthub,

† When yoga was facing its dark days in the early twentieth century, Krishnamacharya needed support to fulfill his mission and preserve the tradition of yoga.... He also knew that he would need help to revive this great Indian tradition. Knowledge of the *Yoga Rahasya* would not be enough, he would need a broad base of knowledge to work from ... in order to present yoga in a proper and just manner. Hungry to learn, he embarked on a journey—a quest—that would take him all over India.

Krishnamacharya's intellectual odyssey began two years later in 1906, when he embarked on an extended period of study with renowned traditional pandits and critical scholars in Mysore, as well as in Varanasi and several other ancient centers of learning in north India. He quickly distinguished himself in several branches † of Hindu philosophy, collecting titles, teaching certificates, and honors in Vedic Studies, Nyaya, Vedanta, and Mimamsa. Wishing to deepen his knowledge of Yoga philosophy, but unable to find university instruction on the subject in Varanasi, he was taken under the wing of the Yoga master Babu Bhagavan Das, who arranged for him to sit as a "private candidate" for a degree in Samkhya-Yoga philosophy at the nearby Patna University. †

Thirsting for a still deeper knowledge of Yoga, Krishnamacharya next traveled to Tibet, where for seven years he was the disciple of a cave-dwelling yogi named Yogeshwara Ramamohana Brahmachari. Shortly after his return, at the request of the Maharaja of Mysore, he took a position as yoga instructor to the royal court. It was here, during his seventeen years at the Mysore Palace's Yogashala, that Krishnamacharya innovated his renowned program of asana and vinyasa and instructed his illustrious pupils B.K.S. Iyengar and K. Pattabhi Jois. Then after the school was shuttered in the early 1950s, he departed for Chennai, where he had been offered a position at the Vivekananda College. In 1961, his son T.K.V. Desikachar gave up a career in engineering to become his pupil. Studying the *Yoga Sutra* with him until Krishnamacharya's death in 1989, Desikachar had a temple erected in his father's honor, which he continues to maintain together with his son Kausthub and other members of the Krishnamacharya Yoga Mandiram's inner circle. †

There are a number of problems with this biographical sketch, which varies in many of its details from one authorized source to another. Most troubling is the absence of any written proof from Krishnamacharya's lifetime of any expertise in Yoga philosophy and the *Yoga Sutra*. Over his five decades of teaching, Krishnamacharya composed four books on yoga and Yoga, two of which during his years at Mysore. The earliest of these, written in the Kannada language, are the recently translated *Yoga Makaranda* ("Emerald of Yoga," 1934) and the partially translated *Yogasanagalu* ("Yoga Postures," 1941). These two works, written in the decades immediately following Krishnamacharya's long years of apprenticeship in Varanasi, Patna, Tibet, and elsewhere, offer scant evidence for his biographers' repeated claims concerning his rigorous training in Yoga philosophy in general and the *Yoga Sutra* in particular.

Apart from a truncated account of the eight-part practice, mainly devoted to the inner and outer restraints, the *Yoga Sutra* is conspicuous by its absence from Krishnamacharya's early works. Virtually no mention is made of the culminating meditative portion of the eight-part practice, and the *Yoga Sutra*'s broader philosophical system is largely ignored. In the rare cases in which it is discussed, it is misrepresented through the use of terminology utterly foreign to Patanjali or his classical commentators. For example, a statement in the "Emerald" that "Yoga is a state of oneness of jivatma (individual soul) and paramatma (universal soul)," is actually a direct quote from "Yajnavalkya's Yoga" (1.44), a south Indian work that synthesized Hatha and Tantric Yoga with Qualified Non-

†

dualist Vedanta philosophy. Upon inspection, it becomes clear that the discussion in the "Emerald" of the eight-part practice, as well as the many links it makes between yoga practice and health, were more directly inspired by this latter work than by the *Yoga Sutra*. Other sources, listed on the first page of the "Emerald," figure far more prominently here; these include works on Hatha Yoga, south Indian Yoga Upanishads, and several other south Indian titles. Furthermore, as Mark Singleton's interviews with a number of Krishnamacharya's pupils from the Mysore Yogashala indicate, none of their master's teachings from that period dealt with the spiritual or philosophical aspects of Yoga. †

How can it be that in spite of his brilliance and extensive training, Krishnamacharya comes across as barely cognizant of the *Yoga Sutra* that had been the presumed object of his Samkhya-Yoga instruction at Patna University as well as of his seven years of discipleship in Tibet with Ramamohana Brahmachari? In fact, between the popularization of Raja Yoga by Vivekananda in the 1890s and the decades of Krishnamacharya's apprenticeship, little had changed in the landscape of Yoga philosophy in India. India's traditional north Indian pandits remained largely unschooled in Yoga philosophy and unaware of the distinctions between the Raja, Hatha, and Tantric Yoga traditions. (Additional proof for this may be found in a work titled *Yogank*, a special issue on Yoga published in 1935 by the Gita Press, which, closely affiliated with † other institutions of traditional learning, was representative of the state of north Indian pandit lore concerning Yoga during those decades.) As we have seen, however, there had been a "*Yoga Sutra* revival" in south India between the sixteenth and eighteenth centuries, and its fading memory may have been the impetus behind Krishnamacharya's interest. In spite of this, Krishnamacharya's Yoga quest always took him north.

According to all of his biographers, Krishnamacharya first traveled to Varanasi. It was precisely during this early period of his studies that the academic field of Yoga studies had begun to flower in an unprecedented fashion, as Indian and Western scholars entered into a vigorous dialogue in matters of Yoga philosophy. James Haughton Woods had come to Mumbai in 1909, where he and a young P. V. Kane (who would later author the monumental *History of Dharmasastra* between 1930 and 1962) read the *Yoga Sutra* together. In his 1914 translation, Woods writes of the assistance he received in Benares from Arthur Venis, the principal of the Government Sanskrit College from 1888 to 1918, in translating a difficult sutra from Patanjali's work. He also praises the scholarship of Mukunda Shastri Adkar, who published critical editions of works on Vedanta and Mimamsa (but not Yoga) there, as well as other Indian philosophers in Pune and Kashmir. In Bengal, an obscure but learned Samkhya renouncer named Hariharananda Aranya was teaching in Kolkata in the early 1910s: we will return to this remarkable figure at the end of this chapter. In the same decade the great Bengali philosopher Surendranath Dasgupta left Kolkata for Cambridge, where he would later write his dissertation on Yoga. The first tome of his five-volume *History of Indian Philosophy*, which included a long section on Yoga philosophy, appeared in 1921.

Another formidable scholar of Indian philosophy was Ganganath Jha, who succeeded Venis as principal of the Government Sanskrit College in Varanasi, serving in that role from 1918 to 1924. Twenty years Krishnamacharya's senior, Jha too was a traditional brahmin who, steeped in the teachings of classical Hindu wisdom, had begun university training at an early age. Jha is notable for having produced an early English translation of the *Yoga Sutra* together with Vyasa's commentary, in 1907. Strongly influenced by Nondualist †
Vedanta thought, he translated the word "yoga" as "communion." Several years earlier, while still a student himself, Jha had translated Vijnanabhikshu's "Short Statement" on the *Yoga Sutra*. Published in †
1894, it was noted with approval by Max Müller in his *Six Systems*.

By the 1920s, Jha had also published extensively on the Upanishads as well as on Mimamsa and Nyaya philosophy. As such, he would have been an ideal Varanasi mentor for Krishnamacharya. So it is that Krishnamacharya's biographers describe the intimate relation- †
ship that developed between Jha and Krishnamacharya during their master's Varanasi years. Recognizing the potential of the young south Indian prodigy, Jha

took a special interest in his destitute young protégé, helping him to win a scholarship and eventually taking him on as a private tutor for his son Amarnath. It was also Jha, we are told, who later directed Krishnamacharya to depart for Tibet to meet Ramamohana Brahmachari, "who would be able to teach him all he wanted to know about yoga,"[1] and Jha who commended Krishnamacharya to the British viceroy in Shimla, from whom he would eventually receive the documents he needed to travel to Tibet.

The obvious question this narrative poses is why Krishnamacharya would have chosen to leave for Patna and Tibet to enhance his knowledge of Yoga philosophy when one of the greatest Indian scholars on the subject was his Varanasi friend and mentor Ganganath Jha? But this question hides the deeper question of when, exactly, all of this was supposed to have taken place. The four family biographies, as well as a recent relatively circumspect 2010 biography by A. G. and Ganesh Mohan, all present divergent chronologies. According to his personal reminiscences, Krishnamacharya either visited Varanasi once and stayed for over a decade, or visited twice, returning to Mysore be

† tween visits. According to a brochure he had self-published in the 1960s, he was in Tibet between 1911 and 1918. The Mohans situate Krishnamacharya's Varanasi years between 1906 and 1911, followed by seven years in Tibet and a brief return visit to Varanasi in

† 1918. The 1982 Desikachar biographical notice simply quotes his father as saying that "he studied with a

Brahmin near Mount Kailash, after all his education in Benares, Allahabad and Calcutta."[2] The 1997, 1998, and 2005 Desikachar biographies place him in Varanasi between 1906 and 1909, and then again between 1914 and 1915 (or 1914 and 1917, followed by seven years in Tibet).

None of these dates permits an encounter of any sort—let alone a strong bond of friendship to have developed—between Krishnamacharya and Jha at any time between 1906 and 1918. The reason is simple. Jha †
was, from 1902 to 1918, professor of Sanskrit at Muir College in Allahabad and did not arrive in Varanasi until 1918, when he succeeded Venis as principal of the Government Sanskrit College. In their later biographies, the Desikachars leave an opening for a possible †
meeting between the two men by evoking a third brief visit to Varanasi in 1922, followed by a series of advanced degrees quickly earned over the following two years, in Kolkata, Allahabad, Varanasi, Vadodara, and Nabadwip. However, the deep friendship and personal relationship that would have preceded this visit and Krishnamacharya's seven years in Tibet is controverted by Krishnamacharya's own 1960s account. It is also chronologically impossible.

Who, then, was Krishnamacharya's Varanasi mentor? The most likely answer may be found on an un- †
dated "Certificate of Commendation" reproduced in Kausthub Desikachar's 2005 biography. That certificate, presented to him by the "celebrated pandits of Benares," lists the names and titles of thirteen tradi-

tional scholars, most of who were also university professors. Many of these scholars' areas of expertise are also indicated on the certificate—and it is striking to note that while four were specialists of grammar and three of Nyaya, with one each specializing in philosophy, astrology, literature, and so forth, none is listed as a specialist in Yoga philosophy. One of the scholars named on this list was Muralidhara Jha, whose official title was "Vice Principal of Government Sanskrit Queen's College." This would have been the person misidentified as Ganganath Jha in the biographies. Had Krishnamacharya come to Varanasi a few years later and actually studied with Ganganath Jha—or if he had studied with Jha's predecessor Arthur Venis and met James Haughton Woods there during the 1910s—his early understanding of Yoga philosophy would have been far more sophisticated and his "Emerald" a more rounded work. Manifestly, this was not the case.

Another chronological problem in Krishnamacharya's academic itinerary concerns Patna University, where he is said to have taken an examination in Samkhya-Yoga philosophy from an unnamed scholar: Patna University was not founded until 1917, and its first examinations not held until 1918. Krishnamacharya could therefore not have studied there before departing for Tibet, and it makes no sense that he would have bothered to sit for a degree in Yoga philosophy at a second-tier university after completing seven years of training with a Himalayan Yoga master.

In the preface to his 1934 "Emerald," Krishnamach- †
arya evokes the "Yoga Sastra in accordance with the
prescribed canons of Pranayama," and later in the same
work he speaks of the "700 asanas he learned from Ramamohan Brahmacari (who knew 7000)."[3] Then, in †
T.K.V. Desikachar's 1982 account of his father's life, in
which mention is first made of Mount Kailash, we are
also told that Krishnamacharya "was instructed in the
use of asana and pranayama for people with sickness by
this great yogi."[4] Later accounts introduce additional
details, details that seemingly take on a life of their
own. Some speak of a lost five-thousand-year-old trea- †
tise titled *Yoga Kuruntam*, which combined the teachings of the *Yoga Sutra* with those of a Vedic sage named
Vamana Rishi. Krishnamacharya would have learned
this work by heart from Brahmachari before discover-
ing a printed version of it in Kolkata, which he transcribed and taught verbatim to Pattabhi Jois before the
work was eaten by ants and lost forever. Not until his
1998 biography, however, does Desikachar speak of the
Yoga Sutra as a component of Brahmachari's teachings
to Krishnamacharya:

> From Sri Ramamohan my father not only learned †
> Patanjali's *Yoga Sutras* by heart, but he also
> learned to chant them with an exactness of pro-
> nunciation, tone, and inflection that echoed as
> nearly as possible their first utterance thousands
> of years earlier.[5]

† The rote memorization and chanting of the *Yoga Sutra* becomes an increasingly prominent theme in the Desikachars' later biographical sketches. By 1961, they tell us, Krishnamacharya had begun to combine chanting with postural practice, always adjusting the number of verses to match the time the student should hold the pose. This was the way he initiated his son into yoga, beginning each lesson with postures and chanting of the *Yoga Sutra*. In his 1982 book, Desikachar writes that he had, over the previous twenty-one years, read through the entire *Yoga Sutra* with Krishnamacharya seven times, noting that "he can play with the Sanskrit words like a good flute player can play the flute,"[6] and correlating his father's skill in chanting to his traditional brahmanic training in Vedic chant.

While his biographers repeatedly stress the depth of Krishnamacharya's personal teachings on *Yoga Sutra* philosophy during his Chennai years from 1961 to the end of his life—teachings that featured exhaustive referencing of the classical commentaries and rigorous glossing of Patanjali's Sanskrit—none of his later writings show any evidence of progress beyond the superficial and inaccurate treatment of the subject found in his 1935 and 1941 works. A Sanskrit-language poem titled the *Yoganjalisaram* ("Essential Benediction of Yoga"), composed by Krishnamacharya in his nineties and published posthumously in 1995, contains no salient references to the *Yoga Sutra*. The "Secret Teaching"—Nathamuni's lost work on Yoga as it had been revealed to the sixteen-year-old Krishnamacharya in 1904, and which Krishnamacharya had purportedly taught to Desikachar between 1963 and 1965—was posthumously published with an English translation by his son in 1998. However, in a 1991 interview, Desikachar denied that the "Secret Teaching" was anything other than a collection of verses on yoga and related subjects composed by Krishnamacharya himself. Its focus on the healing powers of yoga practice bear the stamp of his father's signature approach, but its few vague references to the *Yoga Sutra* are, once again, of little interest. †

In spite of his biographers' considerable efforts, Krishnamacharya's sole verifiable legacy with respect to the *Yoga Sutra* is limited to two areas of practice. The first, which links a sound body to a sound mind and presents the *Yoga Sutra* as a manual for a healthy lifestyle, follows a trend introduced by Vivekananda and expanded upon by nearly every yoga guru of the past hundred years. As his son and grandson repeatedly insist in their biographies, Krishnamacharya was a † great healer whose powers were grounded in his unrivaled understanding of the *Yoga Sutra*. That legacy forms the core of the Krishnamacharya Healing and † Yoga Foundation's therapeutic services, as well as of the well-produced program of online instruction on the *Yoga Sutra* produced by A. G. and Indra Mohan, which is presented under the banner of Svastha Yoga, the "Yoga of Health." There, a wide range of tutorials on the *Yoga Sutra* as a guide for a healthy, happy life features detailed analyses of individual sutras from philosophical, psychological, and physiological standpoints. This, the "medicalization" of Yoga philosophy, has also been embraced by a department within the Government of India's Ministry of Health and Family Welfare, in whose 2006 report we read that

† Yoga is primarily a way of life propounded by Patanjali in a systematic form. It consists of eight components. . . . These steps in the practice of Yoga have potential for improvement of social and personal behavior, improvement of physical health by encouraging better circulation of oxygenated blood in the body, restraining the sense organs and thereby inducing tranquility and serenity of mind. The practice of Yoga prevents psychosomatic disorders/diseases and improves individual resistance and ability to endure stressful situations.[7]

Krishnamacharya's most unique contribution to modern applications of the *Yoga Sutra* lies, however, in the practice of chanting, of accurately reproducing the sounds of the sutras as grounding for postural practice. That an orthodox brahmin should have innovated such a practice is understandable: the accurate chanting of the Veda was central to the traditional education he had received at Parakala. The rationale for Vedic chanting may be found in the Sanskrit term used to denote divine revelation: shruti, "that which was heard" by the ancient Vedic seers, has been communicated orally down the ages to the present day through just this sort of transmission. This is what makes Krishnamacharya's apprenticeship at the feet of Ramamohana Brahmachari—the mysterious sage from a land that time forgot beyond the highest mountains in the world—so essential to his legacy. As the last authentic yogi on the planet, Brahmachari's transmission of the *Yoga Sutra* "with an exactness of pronunciation, tone, and inflection that echoed as nearly as possible their first utterance thousands of years earlier," made Krishnamacharya modern man's sole link to Patanjali's ancient revelation. This also explains his insistence on precise chanting with his son and disciple: without it, that line of transmission would have been severed for all time. And so *Yoga Sutra* chanting has become an integral part of the yoga training offered by Desikachar, Iyengar, and several of their pupils and pupils' pupils—and many are their recordings of hauntingly beautiful chanted renditions of Patanjali's work, in perfect Sanskrit.

In spite of this, there is scant evidence or documentation anywhere in the classical commentarial literature or the historical record to indicate that chanting was ever a component of apprenticeship in the *Yoga Sutra*. While some scholars maintain that Patanjali's work may have been memorized and recited in earlier times—by teachers, disciples, or both—this is entirely speculative. To begin, the *Yoga Sutra* is not the Veda. Unlike the Vedas, which have no author and which were directly revealed to the ancient seers, the *Yoga Sutra*'s author was a human being. In traditional brahmanic education, only shruti is learned by heart, through rote memorization and chanting: without such a precedent, there is no justification for chanting any other sort of work, either sacred or secular.

† Perhaps because he was aware of this, T.K.V. Desikachar provided an original and quite compelling rationale for chanting. In his 1998 biography of his father, he makes a number of statements about chanting the *Yoga Sutra* in accompaniment to or independent of postural practice. As he puts it, chanting, which is as natural and instinctive as the flow of breath, can be used to heal the body, mind, and soul. Here the power of chanting derives not from the meaning of the sutras but rather from a sound quality unique to Sanskrit, "the unique spiritual language of mankind."[8] Chanting can only be learned from a teacher, and Desikachar's teacher was both his father and guru, the person who gave him life as well as the promise of release from suffering existence. By his own admission, his own chanting drove his mother crazy at first, but gradually, "over the years of study I realized that in chanting I was gradually acquiring my father's voice, sounding more like him all the time. Chanting truly entered the rhythms of life, and my teaching."[9] Most important, however, was the link to the past that oral transmission afforded him:

† When I chanted with my father, I was bound to him and his teachings in a unique fashion, just as

in his chanting he was once again linked to his own teacher—and so it stretches back through many centuries of teachers and students, the unbroken line of the *parampara* [lineage]. In our tradition, when we chant, we unite with God, who gave us the language, the practices of Yoga and the wisdom of the Vedas.[10]

Then, in a most interesting move, Desikachar identifies the primordial teacher of all teachers (including of Patanjali) with Ishvara, the Master of Yoga whose identity has been interpreted in so many ways over the centuries:

> As Patanjali relates, God as Ishvara dwells within   † each of us, and our personal conduit is through the *purusha*, the indwelling eternal Perceiver. The *purusha*, however, perceives only through the mind ... In the Yoga system, the mind is considered located in the heart region. This might have something to do with the tradition of learning through sound—the chanting voice of the teacher.[11]

In other words, the medium is the message. There is no need to understand the *Yoga Sutra* analytically; rather, it is sufficient to become a tuning fork for its sound structure, which is nothing other than the voice of the original teacher of Yoga, the God of Yoga himself. This was the voice that Patanjali would have heard, which would have enabled him to compose the *Yoga Sutra*.

Desikachar's is an ingenious position, which posthumously absolves his teacher of any need to clearly explain the meaning of the *Yoga Sutra*—something he appears never to have done, in writing at least. It also fits well with the ongoing fetishization of the *Yoga Sutra* by the current yoga subculture, since it allows for the *Yoga Sutra* to be venerated without being understood.

Although neither Krishnamacharya nor Desikachar have made any mention of it, Vyasa's commentary on sutra 2.1 intimates that he might well have agreed with them. The sutra in question reads: "Practical yoga involves ascetic practice (tapas), study (svadhyaya) and dedication to the Master of Yoga (isvara-pranidhana)." According to Michel Angot, it is the second term in this list, which others have read to mean "self-analysis," that Vyasa interpreted in an altogether unique way. Whereas the meaning of svadhyaya was, in orthodox Vedic interpretation, the personal recitation of the Veda by a brahmin, Vyasa interpreted the term to mean "the repetition of the syllables named pranava (that is, the mantra OM), or of other purifying [texts] or else the study of texts on the subject of release." As Angot argues, the "purifying text" that Vyasa had in mind could not have been anything other than the *Yoga Sutra*, which Vyasa viewed as a teaching originally revealed by a divine Ishvara and only later compiled by the human Patanjali (even if, in his commentary on 1.25, Vyasa identifies Ishvara with the teacher Kapila). Other critical scholars, such as

David Carpenter and Stuart Sarbacker, have similarly argued that *Yoga Sutra* recitation and memorization were intended as practical complements to meditation. Even if, however, one grants that Angot's reading of Vyasa's commentary is a valid one, it nevertheless remains that simply chanting OM or any other Vedic mantra would be fully as effective as reciting the verses of the *Yoga Sutra*. Interestingly, Desikachar relates † that in his teachings Krishnamacharya had identified svadhyaya with postural practice, the very "opening" he needed to link the *Yoga Sutra* to the practice of which he was the undisputed modern master. Many † contemporary yoga gurus, led by Iyengar and Pattabhi Jois, have made similar assertions, affirming that the entire eight-part practice is intrinsic to, or flows directly from, postural practice.

A certain number of the mysteries concerning Krishnamacharya's legacy with respect to the *Yoga Sutra* and Yoga philosophy are dispelled in a Sanskrit- and Tamil-language work titled the *Yogavalli* ("Vine of Yoga"), a teaching his biographers describe as their teacher's most exhaustive commentary on the *Yoga Sutra*, which he would have dictated to an inner circle † of students during the final years of his life. The first volume of the work, which comprises an analysis of the first chapter of the *Yoga Sutra*, was compiled in 1988; the three remaining projected volumes have yet to appear. The "Vine" is a remarkable work, a highly erudite commentary in the ancient commentarial tradition. Intended for the sole use of "insiders"—advanced students enrolled in instruction with the Desikachars and other teachers at the Krishnamacharya Yoga Mandiram in Chennai—it also offers an account of Krishnamacharya's relationship to Yoga philosophy without the cloying sanctimony that characterizes his English-language biographies.

The final pages of the Sanskrit introduction to the "Vine" are most revealing. To begin, the text is presented not as a work by Krishnamacharya, but rather by "the Krishnamacharyans of the Malanka [*sic*] caste living in Madras city."[12] Absent are narratives of chanting in Tibet, of years of academic study in Varanasi and beyond, or of the reception of lost scriptures in a trance. In their place are broad references to the perfected Siddhas of the various Yoga lineages, and an apprenticeship in Yoga undertaken during a Himalayan sojourn. However, the most interesting discussion here concerns the tenth-century Nathamuni's "Secret Teaching." After relating how this teaching had been lost in transmission, the "Vine" then asks, "How is it that the [present] authors... are able to quote its words?"[13] The answer that is given goes straight to the heart of the *Yoga Sutra*, which it quotes: "Knowledge of the past and future arises from perfect discipline of the three transformations of thought" (3.16); and "through direct perception of the cognitive process, one has knowledge of the thoughts of others" (3.19). This is the way of Patanjali's true yogi, whose supernatural powers (which the authors of the "Vine" here say they themselves possess) enabled Krishnamacharya to retrieve lost teachings without recourse to trances, chanting, or university training. In the end, this explanation is far more satisfying and faithful to Patanjali's teachings than the fractured accounts of Krishnamacharya's life his English-language biographies offer. One can only surmise that like the many culture brokers who have preceded them, these authors have been tailoring their message to the sensibilities of their Western audience, and so have preferred to present their guru as a genius and a healer rather than as a true yogi as defined by the *Yoga Sutra*.

This claim of direct access to the past through yogic powers also aligns with positions taken a century earlier by the Theosophists and members of the Brahmo Samaj, who valued the direct revelation received through individual experience, intuition, and introspection over transmission through institutional channels. This comes at a price, however, since it undercuts the importance of the Shrivaishnava lineage that Krishnamacharya's biographers so emphasize. If Krishnamacharya was a direct descendant of Nathamuni, then his guru-disciple lineage ran through Ramanuja, the third Shrivaishnava guru and the greatest star in the Vaishnava philosophical galaxy. It is significant that in their 2011 biography of Krishnamacharya, the Mohans assert that the object of the "Vine" was to interpret the *Yoga Sutra* from the standpoint of the Qualified Nondualist school. To this end, they quote the "Secret Teaching" (1.6–7) as stating that the practices of Qualified Non-Dualism are based entirely on devotion. Therefore ... the practice of Patanjali's yoga should also be done only with devotion. Thus Patanjali's eightfold practice is itself called *bhakti* yoga, or the yoga of devotion, in this context.[14]

Curiously, T.K.V. Desikachar's 1999 text and translation of these same verses from the "Secret Teaching" diverge greatly from the preceding quotation and contain no mention whatsoever of Qualified Nondualism. As we have seen, Ramanuja rejected direct yogic perception as a valid source of knowledge of God or the absolute, which, as he argued, could only be found through scripture. And because Ramanuja's writings have defined Shrivaishnava orthodoxy for nearly a thousand years, claims to Krishnamacharya's special revelation would therefore be rendered null and void.

I cannot leave Krishnamacharya's legacy behind without returning to the place of Tibet—that Shangri-la of many an Orientalist fever dream—in the Krishnamacharya epic. All of Krishnamacharya's biographers locate Krishnamacharya's Yoga master Ramamohana Brahmachari in a cave on the shore of Lake Manasar-
ovar or at the foot of Mount Kailash in Tibet. Yet by Krishnamacharya's own account, in his 1934 "Emerald," his teacher, "who has mastered seven thousand
asanas," was not in Tibet, but rather "in Nepal, living in Muktinarayanakshetram."[15] He makes the same

statement in the original preface to the "Emerald," which was recently discovered in the Mysore Palace archives by Norman Sjoman: "In later years, [the author] had an opportunity of being trained in Yoga Sastra in accordance with the prescribed canons of Pranayama and the several vinyasas by Sri Ramamohan Brahmacari Guru Maharaj of Mukta Narayan Ksetra (Banks of the Gandaki)."[16]

Muktinarayana (also known as Muktinath) is the name of an important Vaishnava shrine situated in northern Nepal, more than two hundred miles away as the crow flies from the Tibetan Mount Kailash. It is difficult to imagine how Krishnamacharya could have made this trek over some of the most rugged terrain in the world. In fact, if we are to follow the 1997 and 2005 Desikachar biographies, Krishnamacharya's trek to Tibet was far more arduous than this. Both accounts underscore the personal relationship he enjoyed with the British viceroy in Shimla. With letters of introduction from Ganganath Jha, he would have met the viceroy and subsequently healed him of a diabetic condition through yoga. "The Viceroy was happy to make arrangements for Krishnamacharya to cross the Himalayas out of India, across Nepal and into Tibet. The expenses of the journey were covered by the British Government."[17] This journey, from Shimla to Tibet via Muktinarayana in Nepal, is said to have taken twenty-one days and covered 211 miles. A glance at a map of the region shows that such an itinerary makes no sense

†

whatsoever, unless traveling from New York to Chicago via Los Angeles makes sense. It would have lengthened his trek by over four hundred miles.

But there is more. Both biographies twice state that † the viceroy requested that Krishnamacharya return to Shimla "once every three months,"[18] so that he could continue with his Yoga study. Let us assume for the sake of argument that after his maiden journey, Krishnamacharya walked directly from Shimla to Tibet, a journey of only four hundred miles, in twenty-one days. If, during those "seven years" in Tibet, he had to be back in Shimla once every three months, then he would have had very little time to spend with either his guru Ramamohana Brahmachari or his pupil the viceroy—perhaps two weeks with each, followed by six weeks of walking and recovery. Further complicating his task would have been relations between British India, China, and Tibet in 1911, which Krishnamacharya himself identifies as the year of his first journey † there. In 1903, the British had invaded Tibet, forcing an "Anglo-Tibetan Agreement" upon Lhasa in 1904. In 1910, the Chinese riposted, with their own military invasion of Lhasa. For the next four years, British subjects were virtually prohibited from entering into western Tibet (where Mount Kailash is located), whether as representatives of the government, trade officials, or "unofficial" British explorers. In other words, any sort of official visa or letter of transit such as Krishnamacharya may have been provided by the viceroy in

Shimla would have been worthless. Now, it is true that Chinese power collapsed in central Tibet in 1912, such that after 1914 the whole issue was more or less forgotten for two decades. Therefore, if, as his late biographies have it, he did not leave for Tibet until 1917, then such a journey might have been "politically" possible, but still highly implausible. †

In his 2011 article, Fernando Pagès Ruiz notes that Krishnamacharya was a "shrewd card player." So was †
James Bond, albeit not before the 1950s. Closer to the young Krishnamacharya's time, an English author used India and Tibet as the setting for a tale of another secret agent. This was Rudyard Kipling, whose 1901 novel *Kim* featured an Indian waif (Kim), a Shimla-based British spymaster, a spy (Lurgan Sahib, codenamed E23) who put on the guise of a yogi to pass incognito, and a Tibetan holy man. Kim's training in Shimla, which prepared him to be an operative in the "Great Game," involved rote memorization (of objects, in the "Jewel Game" or "Kim's Game"). Now let us suppose for a moment that Krishnamacharya's viceroy in Shimla was a spymaster, and his frequent journeys from India to Tibet in the guise of a yogi were conducted to carry memorized intelligence back from an agent posing as a holy man in Tibet. The symmetry is compelling and the plot no less implausible than the Just So stories of Krishnamacharya's biographies. Truth is stranger than fiction, but where is the truth in all of this? The mind boggles.

Tirumalai Krishnamacharya was a remarkably complex figure, a larger than life yogi in a diminutive body whose legacy in some way extends to nearly every one of the tens of millions of contemporary practitioners who take to their yoga mats on a daily basis. Even if, as one of his biographers has written, several details of his life "lie shrouded in myth," and even if the chronologies he and his biographers have proposed have enough holes in them to fill the Albert Hall, one cannot deny Krishnamacharya's pivotal role in the history of modern understandings of the *Yoga Sutra*. It is my belief that Krishnamacharya did eventually train his massive intellect upon the *Yoga Sutra*, and that the highly sophisticated "Vine" did originate with him—but that he did not come to Patanjali's work until relatively late in life, during his Chennai years; that is, at about the same time as his former pupil (and prime contender in terms of legacy) B.K.S. Iyengar. I seriously doubt, however, that he was ever the Frodo Baggins of modern Yoga that his biographers have made him out to be.

Here it is useful to compare these reconstructions of Krishnamacharya's life with that of Hariharananda Aranya, his elder by twenty years. The son of a wealthy Kolkata landowner, Aranya, after a few years of college training in Sanskrit, "chanced upon a copy of an ancient text on Samkhya-Yoga in a library. It resulted in his ... taking the vow of a sannyasin (renouncer)"[19] and withdrawing, in 1892, to the caves of the Barabar Hills in what is now the eastern Indian state of

Jharkhand. There he spent six years in contemplation on the twenty-five principles of Samkhya, eventually "gain[ing] mastery over his mind, which is Yoga." It may have been during these years that he received instruction from Swami Triloki Aranya, who, as he claimed, belonged to a lineage extending back to Patanjali himself. After a decade of wandering, he returned in the early 1910s to Kolkata, where, in addition to giving instruction in Samkhya and Yoga philosophy, he published a Bengali-language commentary on the *Yoga Sutra* in 1911. Titled the *Bhasvati* ("Dawning Sun"), it was the first commentary since Bhoja's eleventh-century "Royal Sun" to fully respect and argue for the philosophical principles of Samkhya-Yoga enshrined in Patanjali's work. Following which, Aranya returned to the Barabar Caves, where he gathered a small following of disciples who, at his request, sealed him into a cave in 1926. He would remain there, receiving food and giving teachings through a window in the cave, until his death in 1947. Over the years, the "Dawning Sun" has become a classic, going into several editions in Hindi as well as English. Truly a masterwork, it and Aranya's many other Bengali- and Sanskrit-language publications are the products of the great mind of an authentic scholar-practitioner.

† †

Yoga Sutra 2.0

According to popular Jewish lore, two Jews will produce at least three opinions on any given subject. So it
also is with scholars with respect to the *Yoga Sutra*.
Does kaivalyam ("isolation"), the goal of Yoga prac-
† tice, mean that the practitioner dies to the world? For
Yohanan Grinshpon, the answer is yes: "Yoga requires
that the person disintegrate.... It is the absolute, un-
† fathomable end, the end of ends."[1] For Chris Chapple
and Ian Whicher, the answer is no: Yoga entails enlightened engagement with the world; while Shyam
Ranganathan goes so far as to say that the *Yoga Sutra* is
a work of moral philosophy, guiding men to become
morally perfect in the world. Is the *Yoga Sutra* an incoherent patchwork of prior Yoga traditions stitched together by Patanjali, or is it a single, homogeneous com-
† pilation? Whereas several scholars have argued that
the *Yoga Sutra* was patched together from no fewer
than five or six separate texts, Georg Feuerstein has co-
gently demonstrated that it was a unified discourse on

"meditation practice" (kriya yoga) with a long quote on the eight-part practice inserted into its second and third chapters. Was there ever a Yoga philosophy that existed independent of Samkhya? While Feuerstein † has argued vigorously in support of this hypothesis, the general scholarly consensus since Colebrooke has been that Yoga philosophy is nothing more than "Samkhya with Ishvara."

Of late, some of the greatest scholarly controversy has whirled around the identities of Patanjali and Vyasa. In chapter 1, we saw Edwin Bryant echoing what most critical scholars have assumed for nearly two centuries—that since the fourth century, all of Patanjali's readers have read the *Yoga Sutra* through the lens of Vyasa's "Commentary." Many, including Bry- † ant, have maintained that the *Yoga Sutra* was learned and transmitted through rote recitation, after the fashion of Krishnamacharya and his followers. Challenging both of these assumptions is the claim, made by a number of scholars since the early twentieth century, but most recently articulated with the greatest clarity by Philipp André Maas, that (1) there never was a Vyasa, only a Patanjali; (2) the sutras together with the "Commentary" formed a single, unified work; and (3) the name of that work was not *Yoga Sutra*, but rather *Yoga Shastra* (the "Teaching on Yoga").

Until 1929, all critical scholars had identified Patanjali's work as the *Yoga Sutra* and assumed that Vyasa, its earliest commentator, was a near contemporary of Patanjali—a student perhaps—who composed a skeleton key to his master's work in order to make it more comprehensible to all. Like Patanjali, Vyasa's is a name that has been attributed either to several historical figures or to a single individual who lived for thousands of years. According to Hindu tradition, Vyasa—whose name means the "Editor" or "Divider"—divided the original revealed Veda into the four great works of the Vedic canon: the *Rig Veda, Yajur Veda, Sama Veda*, and *Atharva Veda* (for this reason, he is also referred to as "Veda-Vyasa"). Some time later—a day? a year? a millennium? ten thousand years?—he composed the *Mahabharata* epic, writing himself into the plot as the progenitor of both of the warring family lines in that epic's cataclysmic battle. Finally, midway through the fourth century, Vyasa redacted the "Commentary" on the *Yoga Sutra*. But was there a historical figure behind this name and the legend that went with it? Seeking to separate this historical Vyasa from the mythic "Divider" of the Vedas and the *Mahabharata*, a number of critical scholars have argued that the "Editor" of the *Yoga Sutra* may have been a certain Vindhyavasin, a renowned Samkhya philosopher from the fourth or fifth century.

However, some have suggested that this is not the only possible scenario. Given that Vyasa's name simply means the "Editor," they argue, Vyasa may simply have been a title attributed to Patanjali by none other than himself. In other words, Vyasa could have simply been a nom de plume Patanjali adopted for the purpose of writing what is known as an "auto-commentary" on his collected aphorisms. This raises another problem, however, because Patanjali-Vyasa's interpretations of several sutras (including the sutras on Ishvara) clearly contradict the patent meaning of the sutras themselves. In response to this, Johannes Bronkhorst suggested in 1985 that one could have it both ways by simply revising one's view of Patanjali's role in the composition of the *Yoga Sutra*. This hypothesis, which † has been gaining ground among critical scholars, maintains that our author "brought the *Yoga Sutra* together, perhaps from different sources, and wrote a commentary which in some cases demonstrably deviated from the original intention of the *sutras*."[2] In other words, Patanjali was more a compiler-commentator than the founder of a distinct philosophical school, and more of a theoretician than a person having any practical yogic experience.

But this is not all. Already in 1931, Hermann Jacobi † had noted that a significant number of early and important Indian scholars and commentators had identified Patanjali as the author of a work entitled the *Yoga Shastra*. Maas expands on this insight by observing that relatively few *Yoga Sutra* manuscripts simply consist of Patanjali's 195 stand-alone aphorisms sans Vyasa's commentary. Far more often, the aphorisms appear embedded in the text of the original commentary, with nearly all carrying the following notation in their colophon: "This has been Patanjali's authoritative † 'Teaching on Yoga' (*Yoga Shastra*), an exposition of Samkhya (samkhya-pravachana)." Virtually no manuscript colophons ever mention a distinct "Commentary" (Bhashya) or commentator (Vyasa). In other words, most *Yoga Sutra* manuscripts are *Yoga Shastra* manuscripts, which means that for the past two hundred years at least, people have been calling this text by the wrong name.

† Maas has traced outside references to the *Yoga Shastra* to as far back as 650 CE. He has also found that prior to Madhava's 1340 CE "Compendium," no Indian work had ever evoked Patanjali and Vyasa as separate authors of a root text (called the *Yoga Sutra*) and a separate "Commentary." Maas then carries his argument one step further, challenging the notion that the
† medieval sources had ever viewed Yoga philosophy as distinct from Samkhya philosophy. Prior to the sixteenth century, he argues, the school to which the *Yoga Shastra* was assigned was never called Yoga, but rather Samkhya-Yoga. At the very most, Yoga was considered to be a subschool of Samkhya, known since the twelfth century, as we have seen, as "Samkhya with Ishvara." Therefore, the very idea that one could read, recite, or memorize the *Yoga Shastra*'s 195 aphorisms independent of the roughly 1,100 stanzas of Samkhya philosophy in which they are embedded, is simply misguided.

The divergences that Bronkhorst noted, between the expressed meanings of a dozen sutras and their explanation in the accompanying commentary, open the way to another theory on the relationship between Patanjali and Vyasa. Here I am speaking of a fact I alluded to in chapter 1. To wit, that the language of the sutras is often closer to what has been termed "Buddhist Hybrid Sanskrit" than to the classical Sanskrit that was the norm in Hindu scripture and commentary. With this, we must acknowledge the presence of a twelve-thousand-pound elephant in the room, the room being the *Yoga Sutra* and the elephant Buddhist philosophy, which dominated the Indian philosophical arena throughout the first five hundred years of the Common Era. The Buddhists of the period were quick to contest viewpoints that conflicted with their own, yet they are nearly entirely silent with regard to the *Yoga Sutra*. Why would this have been the case? Why would the Buddhist heavyweights not have attacked Patanjali's work?

A possible explanation is that the Buddhists found the sutras to be commensurate with their doctrines—that is, they considered the *Yoga Sutra* to be a Buddhist work. Since scholars began debating this possibility in 1900, momentum has been building in support of this hypothesis. A very exciting recent development is a tract on the yogic path to liberation recently brought to light by Dominik Wujastyk. Embedded in the *Charaka Samhita*, this passage likely predates the *Yoga Sutra* by at least a hundred years. Most interesting, as Wujastyk notes, the Yoga system propounded in this teaching "has closer links to Vaisesika philosophy than to the Samkhya of Patanjali's system," and is to be placed "squarely within the tradition of Buddhist mindfulness meditation."[3]

† An alternative hypothesis, which Dasgupta first voiced in 1922, maintains that the *Yoga Sutra*'s entire fourth chapter is a late addition, appended precisely in order to "secur[e] the strength of the Yoga [system] from the supposed attacks of Buddhist metaphysics."[4] In noting Dasgupta's position, Gerald James Larson raises another issue, which brings us back to the question of the relationship of the author of the *Yoga Sutra* to that of its original commentary. As Larson puts it,

† my puzzlement has to do with the opposite problem, that is, how this terminology that is common to the Y[oga] S[utra] and Buddhist Abhidharma relates to the old Samkhya philosophy. What is striking is that all of these common terms used in the Y[oga] S[utra] and Buddhist textual environments are totally absent in Samkhya textual environments.[5]

At about the same time as Larson was expressing his puzzlement, Mikel Burley was offering a possible solution to it. Following a careful reading of the sutras of
† Patanjali's fourth chapter, Burley concluded that it was not Patanjali who was taking issue with Buddhist positions but rather Vyasa and his later subcommentators. Here we see Burley driving Patanjali and Vyasa apart, in much the same way as Bronkhorst had done in his 1985 study when he noted divergences between the intended meanings of a dozen sutras and their accompanying commentary. On the basis of these data, one can

only conclude that the author of the *Yoga Sutra* and its "Commentary" could *not* have been one and the same person.

Of course, this flies in the face of Maas's demonstration that Vyasa never existed, and that Patanjali composed a work titled the *Yoga Shastra*, which comprised both the "Yoga Sutra" and an auto-commentary. Maas is one of the two current *Yoga Sutra* specialists most capable of thinking out of the box: the other is Michel Angot, who presents his counterhypothesis in the strongest of terms. Briefly stated, Angot has theorized † that the first three chapters of the *Yoga Sutra* were a "Buddhist" work written by Patanjali, perhaps no later than the first century of the Common Era; but that the work's final chapter was written in its entirety by a Hindu named Vyasa, perhaps as late as the sixth or seventh century. (Although Angot does not mention it, this might also explain why the Arabic and Old Javanese versions omit the *Yoga Sutra*'s fourth chapter.) Angot begins with the language of the *Yoga Sutra* aphorisms, noting that "the work becomes quite coherent † if one works from the meaning that certain words have in '[Buddhist] Hybrid Sanskrit,' but not in classical Sanskrit."[6] For Angot, Vyasa's would not even have been the earliest commentary on the *Yoga Sutra*: it is simply the earliest surviving commentary.

> Why was it [the earlier commentary] replaced? †
> Since we do not have it, we can only offer a set of
> hypotheses. Vyasa's commentary has two features

that are interesting in this regard: it is overtly hostile toward Buddhism in a time of open war between Brahmins and [Buddhist and Jain] Sramanas . . . clearly, it is offered to Brahmins and to Brahmins alone. Vyasa speaks of Brahmins as the users and therefore the target audience of the work. . . . So I can imagine that the original commentary, which would have been more ecumenical, was replaced by a commentary written by a Brahmin for Brahmins, when this latter group, seeing its primacy being challenged by these [Buddhist and Jain] latecomers, counterattacked.[7]

† In other words, Vyasa's was not so much a commentary as a "translation"—if not a "hostile takeover"—of a fundamentally Buddhistic work into a Hindu, if not orthodox brahmin, idiom. If Patanjali was addressing himself to Yoga connoisseurs in an effort to synthesize distinct but well-founded and legitimate views, Vyasa's goal was to explain the *Yoga Sutra* to brahmins who were not necessarily familiar with Yoga.

† Patanjali's references are entirely non-Hindu: in fact, he neglects, whether voluntarily or involuntarily, the entirety of their sacred literature (the Vedas) . . . Vyasa's are entirely different: he lived in the sixth, or perhaps the seventh century. . . . Vyasa's references come from the Puranas. . . . In short, between Patanjali and Vyasa, one passes from the end of the Vedic period to that of Hinduism in its

brahminical form. Furthermore, Patanjali did not live at "the end of the Vedic period," but rather at a time in which new spiritual idioms, most notably those of Buddhism and Jainism, were emerging and taking shape. And yoga, which was neither Vedic nor Hindu in its origins, had now forced its way into the Hindu world [through Vyasa's fourth chapter and "Commentary"].[8]

There is no way to square the circle between Maas's and Angot's positions. Vyasa could not have both been Patanjali's alias and a person from an entirely different time and religious background. At the same time, if one proceeds from the premises to the conclusions of their respective arguments, both are entirely plausible. In either case, we can be certain of a number of things: that the book you have been reading is the reception history of a work that may or may not be titled the *Yoga Sutra*; that the author of that work may or may not have been named Patanjali; and that that work may or not have been the subject of an original and separate commentary by a person probably not named Vyasa.

No doubt critical scholars will go on grinding the *Yoga Sutra* and their own interpretive models down to a powder. They cannot help themselves: Descartes' principle of methodological skepticism, first articulated in a 1641 work titled *Meditations*, is part of †   scholarly DNA. It is nonetheless worth noting that Descartes chose the unusual term "meditation" for the process by means of which the philosopher should eventually come to an introspective understanding of the very grounds for true cognition. In this, his project was uncannily similar to Patanjali's: the quest for authenticity is to be carried out through introspection.

This message clearly resonated with South Asian populations between the seventh and twelfth centuries, the period in which the *Yoga Sutra* enjoyed the status of a classic. And now, after a hiatus of nearly a millennium Patanjali's work has—improbably, miraculously—recovered that status. This being said, *Yoga Sutra* 2.0 has little in common with the original version. Its readership is no longer restricted to those who know Sanskrit: at the time of this writing (summer 2013), the work has been translated into no fewer than forty-six languages. Its readership is not restricted to an intellectual elite, the persons who debated its teachings in their commentaries, but is rather open to anyone with what is called "a yoga practice." Furthermore, as we have seen, many in the massive, vibrant yoga subculture have no use for translations or commentaries (to say nothing of the writings of critical scholars), preferring to read—or more properly speaking, recite— Patanjali's work in the original Sanskrit. Its truth, and by extension the authenticity of their own yoga practice, lies in the simple fact that it exists and that its words are there, recoverable across space and time through the simple act of performance. For many of my friends in the yoga subculture, this is a source of solace and inspiration.

In the course of the three years during which I have been working on this book, a new development, perhaps the most significant development in the modern history of Yoga, has been taking shape—in India. There, a charismatic homespun yoga guru named Yog Rishi Swami Ramdev has been transforming a north Indian yoga center featuring large-scale "yoga camps" into a populist political movement. Called the "Patanjali Yoga Shrine and Heavenly Yoga Temple," the center's website contains links to sister organizations in Britain and the United States, to a Patanjali Research Park, a Patanjali Food and Herbal Park, and so forth, and to videos of Ramdev's many Hindi-language sermons on the *Yoga Sutra*. Millions of his followers also follow his sermons and yoga demonstrations on television, both in India and abroad (including in Los Angeles, where I live). †

Over the past three years, Ramdev has often journeyed—with the backing, it is rumored, of various Hindu nationalist organizations—to Delhi where he has organized massive anticorruption rallies and undertaken highly publicized hunger strikes to reform India's political system. He explains his newfound transition, from the yogic body to the body politic, in the clearest of terms: "We clean up our bodies... Then we will clean up our democracy!"[9] At long last, the *Yoga Sutra* has been returned to its north Indian homeland, and this time the revolution is being televised. †

Complete references to the works cited in the notes may be found in the online bibliography to this volume, which can be accessed through http://press.princeton.edu/titles/10193 .html.

CHAPTER 1 Reading the *Yoga Sutra* in the Twenty-First Century

1. Sir Monier Monier-Williams, *A Sanskrit-English Dictionary: Etymologically and Philologically Arranged with Special Reference to Cognate Indo-European Languages* (London: Oxford University Press, 1899; reprint, Delhi: Motilal Banarsidass, 1984), 856–57.
2. Edwin Bryant, *The Yoga Sutras of Patanjali* (New York: North Point Press, 2009), xxxviii.

CHAPTER 2 Patanjali, the *Yoga Sutra*, and Indian Philosophy

1. Rajendralal Mitra, *The Yoga Aphorisms of Patanjali* (Kolkata: Asiatic Society of Bengal, 1883), 9 (commenting on *Yoga Sutra* 1.4). He further refers to this

principle at pages 171 and 194, commenting on *Yoga Sutra* 4.3 and 4.22.

2. Bryant, *The Yoga Sutras of Patanjali*, 288; James Haughton Woods, *The Yoga-System of Patanjali* (Cambridge, MA: Harvard University Press, 1914), xiii.

3. Guruling Deva, ed., *Virasaivanandacandrika sriman-narnajana Maritondarya Sivayogiviracita* (Hubli: Somashekhar Shastri, 1936), 448.

4. B.K.S. Iyengar, *Light on the Yoga Sutras of Patanjali* (New Delhi: Harper Collins, 1993), 2.

5. Mikel Burley, *Classical Samkhya and Yoga: An Indian Metaphysics of Experience* (New York: Routledge, 2007), 85–86.

6. Richard King, *Indian Philosophy: An Introduction to Hindu and Buddhist Thought* (Edinburgh: Edinburgh University Press, 1999), 210.

CHAPTER 3 Henry Thomas Colebrooke and the Western "Discovery" of the *Yoga Sutra*

1. Rosane Rocher, "British Orientalism in the Eighteenth Century," in *Orientalism and the Postcolonial Predicament: Perspectives on South Asia*, ed. Carol Breckenridge and Peter van der Veer (Philadelphia: University of Pennsylvania Press, 1993), 225. Rocher's major work on Colebrooke and the Orientalists, which appeared after this book had gone into production, is noted in the bibliography as Rosane Rocher and Ludo Rocher, *The Making of Western Indology: Henry Thomas Colebrooke and the East India Company* (New York: Routledge, 2012).

2. Sir Charles Wilkins, *The Bhagavat-Geeta, or Dialogues*

of Kreeshna *and* Arjoon; *in Eighteen Lectures with Notes* (London: C. Nourse, 1785), 142, note to p. 73.

3. Henry Thomas Colebrooke, *Miscellaneous Essays*, 2 vols. (London: W. H. Allen, 1837), 1: 252–53.
4. Ibid., 1: 235, 236, 253.
5. J. Cockburn Thomson, *The Bhagavad-Gita; or, A Discourse between Krishna and Arjuna on Divine Matters* (Hertford: Stephen Austin, 1855), cxxix.
6. Fitzedward Hall, *A Contribution towards an Index to the Bibliography of the Indian Philosophical Systems* (Kolkata: C. B. Lewis, 1859), xi.
7. Mitra, *The Yoga Aphorisms of Patanjali*, lvi.
8. Romesh Chunder Dutt, *A History of Civilization in Ancient India*, vol. 1 (Kolkata: Thacker, Spink, 1889), 288.
9. Colebrooke, *Miscellaneous Essays*, 1: 250–51.
10. Colonel James Tod, *Annals and Antiquities of Rajast'han*, 2 vols., with a preface by Douglas Sladen (London: H. Milford, 1829, 1832; reprint, 1957; London: Routledge and Kegan Paul, 1972), 1957 edition, 562–63.
11. William Ward, *View of the History, Literature, and Religion of the Hindoos*, 3rd ed., 4 vols. (London: Black, Kingsbury, Barbury, and Allen, 1820), 4: 500–501.
12. Colebrooke, *Miscellaneous Essays*, 1: 336.
13. J[ames] R. Ballantyne, trans., *The Aphorisms of the Yoga Philosophy of Patanjali with Illustrative Extracts from the Commentary by Bhoja Raja* (Allahabad: Presbyterian Missionary Press, 1852), ii.
14. Mitra, *The Yoga Aphorisms of Patanjali*, xc.

15. Friedrich Max Müller, *The Six Systems of Indian Philosophy* (New York: Longmans, Green, 1899), xx.

CHAPTER 4   *Yoga Sutra* Agonistes

1. Wilhelm Halbfass, *India and Europe: An Essay in Understanding* (Albany: State University of New York Press, 1988), 75.
2. Herbert Herring, ed. and trans., G.W.F. Hegel: *On the Episode of the Mahabharata Known by the Name Bhagavad-Gita by Wilhelm von Humboldt, Berlin 1826* (New Delhi: Indian Council of Philosophical Research, 1995), 33.
3. Ibid., 41.
4. Ibid., 25, 27.
5. Ibid., 29.
6. Colebrooke, *Miscellaneous Essays*, 1: 361.
7. Herring, *On the Episode of the Mahabharata*, 61, 65, 71, 73.
8. Robert Bernasconi, "With What Must the History of Philosophy Begin? Hegel's Role in the Debate on the Place of India within the History of Philosophy," in *Hegel's History of Philosophy*, ed. David A. Duquette (Albany: State University of New York Press, 2003), 45–46.

CHAPTER 5   Rajendralal Mitra

1. Ram Shankar Bhattacharya, *An Introduction to the Yogasutra* (Delhi: Bharatiya Vidya Prakasana, 1985), 32.
2. Mitra, *The Yoga Aphorisms of Patanjali*, lii–lv.

3. Ibid., lxxix.

4. Ibid., lvi.

5. Ibid., 208.

6. Ibid., lxi.

7. Ibid., lxi.

CHAPTER 6   The Yoga of the Magnetosphere

1. Mark Singleton, *Yoga Body: The Origins of Modern Posture Practice* (New York: Oxford University Press, 2010), 77.

2. Annie Besant, "An Introduction to Yoga," 1907, found at http://www.anandgholap.net/Introduction_To _Yoga-AB.htm, para. 52.

3. Alice Bailey, *The Light of the Soul, Its Science and Effect: A Paraphrase of the Yoga Sutras of Patanjali* (New York: Lucis, 1927), vii.

4. Ernest Wood, *The Occult Training of the Hindus* (Sydney and Chicago: Theosophical Publishing House, 1932). Reprinted as *The Seven Schools of Yoga: An Introduction* (Chennai: Theosophical Publishing House, 1976), 1976 edition, 12.

5. Helena Petrovna Blavatsky, "Comments on a Treatise on the Yoga Philosophy," in *H. P. Blavatsky Collected Writings*, vol. 2 (Wheaton, IL: Theosophical Press, 1967), 462, found at http://www.katinkahesselink .net/blavatsky/articles/v2/y1880_058.htm.

6. Jason Birch, "The Meaning of Hatha in Early Hatha-yoga," *Journal of the American Oriental Society* 131, no. 4 (2011): 543.

CHAPTER 7   Swami Vivekananda and the
Mainstreaming of the *Yoga Sutra*

1. Max Müller, *The Six Systems of Indian Philosophy*,
   xviii–xix.
2. Monier-Williams, *A Sanskrit-English Dictionary*, 856.
3. Elizabeth De Michelis, *A History of Modern Yoga:
   Patañjali and Western Esotericism* (New York and
   London: Continuum, 2004), 89.
4. Singleton, *Yoga Body*, 169.
5. D. H. Killingly, "*Yoga-Sutra* IV, 2–3 and Vivekananda's
   Interpretation of Evolution," *Journal of Indian
   Philosophy* 18 (1990): 168.
6. Swami Vivekananda, *The Complete Works*, 9 vols.
   (Kolkata: Advaita Ashram, 1907–97), 1907, 1: 122,
   found at http://www.advaitaashrama.org/cw/content
   .php.
7. Shrinivasa Iyangar, ed. and trans., *Hathayogapradipika
   of Svatmaraman: With the Commentary of Brahmananda* (Mumbai: Theosophical Publication Fund, 1893;
   Chennai: Adyar, 1972), 1972 edition, 22.
8. J[ohn] N[icol] Farquhar, *Modern Religious Movements in India* (New York: Macmillan, 1915; Delhi:
   Munshiram Manoharlal, 1967), 1967 edition, 438.
9. Swami Vivekananda, *Raja-Yoga: Conquering the
   Internal Nature* (Kolkata: Advaita Ashram, 1896; rev.
   ed., New York: Ramakrishna-Vivekananda Center,
   1973), 1973 edition, 18.
10. Vivekananda, *The Complete Works*, 1907, 1: 257.
11. Vivekananda, *Raja-Yoga*, 207–8.
12. Bhagwan Rajneesh, *Yoga: The Science of the Soul* (New
    York: St. Martin's Griffin, 1984), 7.

13. Killingly, "*Yoga-Sutra* IV, 2–3 and Vivekananda's Interpretation of Evolution," 161.

14. Woods, *The Yoga-System of Patanjali,* 304; T. S. Rukmani, trans., *The Yogavarttika of Vijnanabhiksu,* 4 vols. (Delhi: Munshiram Manoharlal, 1981–89), 4: 13.

15. Mark Singleton, "The Classical Reveries of Modern Yoga: Patanjali and Constructive Orientalism," in *Yoga in the Modern World: Contemporary Perspectives,* ed. Mark Singleton and Jean Byrne (London: Routledge, 2008), 80.

CHAPTER 8 The *Yoga Sutra* in the Muslim World

1. Thomas Dahnhardt, *Change and Continuity in Indian Sufism: A Naqshbandi-Mujaddidi Branch in the Hindu Environment* (New Delhi: D. K. Printworld, 2002), 84.

2. Colonel H[enry] S[ullivan] Jarrett, *The Ain i Akbari by Abul Fazl-i-Allami, Translated from the Original Persian,* vol. 3 (Kolkata: Baptist Mission Press, 1894), 183.

3. Ibid., 186.

4. Ibid., 186–87.

5. Vincent A. Smith, *The Oxford History of India,* 3rd ed., edited by Percival Spear (Oxford: Oxford University Press, 1958), 209.

6. Shlomo Pines and Tuvia Gelblum, "Al-Biruni's Arabic Version of Patanjali's Yogasutra: A Translation of His Second Chapter and a Comparison with Related Texts," *Bulletin of the School of Oriental and African Studies* 40, no. 3 (1977): 522.

7. Shlomo Pines and Tuvia Gelblum, "Al-Biruni's Arabic

Version of Patanjali's Yogasutra: A Translation of His
First Chapter and a Comparison with Related Texts,"
Bulletin of the School of Oriental and African Studies
29, no. 2 (1966): 304–5.

CHAPTER 9 The *Yoga Sutra* Becomes a Classic

1. Edward. C. Sachau, *Alberuni's India: An Account of the
   Religion, Philosophy, Literature, Geography, Chronol-
   ogy, Astronomy, Customs, Laws, and Astrology of India
   about 1030*, 2 vols. (London: Kegan Paul, Trench,
   Trübner, 1910; Delhi: Munshiram Manoharlal, 1983),
   1983 edition, 191–92.

CHAPTER 10 Ishvara

1. Swami Vivekananda, "On Professor Max Müller,"
   Brahmavadin, June 6, 1896, found at http://www
   .ramakrishnavivekananda.info/vivekananda/vol
   ume_4/writings_prose/on_professor_max_muller
   .htm.
2. Max Müller, *The Six Systems of Indian Philosophy*, xx.
3. Ibid., 408–9.
4. Olivier Lacombe, *L'absolu selon le Vedanta* (Paris: Paul
   Geuthner, 1966), 268; Arion Roşu, *Les conceptions
   psychologiques dans les textes médicaux indiens* (Paris:
   De Boccard, 1978), 11n5.
5. Barbara Stoler Miller, *Yoga: Discipline of Freedom*
   (Berkeley: University of California Press, 1996), 36.
6. Max Müller, *The Six Systems of Indian Philosophy*, 426.
7. Arthur Berriedale Keith, "Some Problems of Indian

Philosophy," *Indian Historical Quarterly* 8, no. 3
(1932): 434.

CHAPTER 11   Journeys East, Journeys West

1. Peter Heehs, *The Lives of Sri Aurobindo* (New York: Columbia University Press, 2008), 239.
2. P. V. Kane, *History of Dharmasastra*, vol. 5, part 2 (1962; Pune: Bhandarkar Oriental Research Institute, 1977), 1465.
3. Mircea Eliade, *Yoga, Immortality, and Freedom*, trans. Willard R. Trask (New York: Bollingen Foundation, 1958), 361.
4. Swami Prabhavananda and Christopher Isherwood, *How to Know God* (1953; Hollywood, CA: Vedanta Press, 1971), 15.
5. William H. O'Donnell, ed., *W. B. Yeats: Later Essays* (New York: Charles Scribner's Sons, 1994), 175.
6. Ibid., 175.
7. Arthur Koestler, *The Yogi and the Commissar* (New York: Macmillan, 1945), 246.
8. Found at http://www.mum.edu/RelId/606573 /ISvars/default/TM-Sidhi_Program.htm. See also http://www.minet.org/mantras.html and http:// www.permanentpeace.org/technology/yogic_flying .html.

CHAPTER 12   The Strange Case of T. M. Krishnamacharya

1. A. G. Mohan and Ganesh Mohan, *Krishnamacharya: His Life and Teachings* (Boston: Shambhala, 2010), 3.

2. T.K.V. Desikachar, *The Yoga of T. Krishnamacharya* (Chennai: Krishnamacharya Yoga Mandiram, 1982), 8.

3. N[orman] E. Sjoman, *The Yoga Tradition of the Mysore Palace* (New Delhi: Abhinav Publications, 1996), 51; Nandini Ranganathan and Lakshmi Ranganathan, *Yoga Makaranda or Yoga Saram (The Essence of Yoga)*, 2007, 25, found at http://grimmly2007.blogspot.com /2011/04/krishnamacharyas-yoga-makaranda-at-last .html.

4. Desikachar, *The Yoga of T. Krishnamacharya*, 30.

5. T.K.V. Desikachar and R. H. Cravens, *Health, Healing, and Beyond: Yoga and the Living Tradition of Krishnamacharya* (New York: Aperture, 1998), 43.

6. Desikachar, *The Yoga of T. Krishnamacharya*, 6; Kausthub Desikachar, *The Yoga of the Yogi: The Legacy of T. Krishnamacharya* (Chennai: Krishnamacharya Yoga Mandiram, 2005), 190.

7. Joseph S. Alter, "Endpiece," *Asian Medicine: Tradition and Modernity*, Special Yoga Issue, edited by Mark Singleton, 3, no. 1 (2007): 177.

8. Desikachar and Cravens, *Health, Healing, and Beyond*, 158.

9. Ibid., 159.

10. Ibid., 160.

11. Ibid., 106.

12. *Yogavalli*, vol. 1, privately printed, but unpublished work by "the Krishnamacharyas living in Madras city," 1988, 22.

13. Ibid., 26–27.

14. Mohan and Mohan, *Krishnamacharya: His Life and Teachings*, 135.

15. Ranganathan and Ranganathan, *Yoga Makaranda or Yoga Saram (The Essence of Yoga)*, 25.

16. Sjoman, *The Yoga Tradition of the Mysore Palace*, 51.

17. T.K.V. Desikachar, *Sri Krishnamacharya the Purnacarya* (New York: Aperture, 1997), 25.

18. Ibid., 25, 27–28; Desikachar, *The Yoga of the Yogi*, 48, 52.

19. "Biography of Hariharananda Aranya," found at the "Kapil Math" website, www.samkhyayoga-darshana.com.

CHAPTER 13   *Yoga Sutra* 2.0

1. Yohanan Grinshpon, *Silence Unheard* (Albany: State University of New York Press, 2002), 1.

2. Johannes Bronkhorst, "Patanjali and the Yoga Sutras," *Studien zur Indologie und Iranistik* 10 (1985): 203.

3. Dominik Wujastyk, "The Path to Liberation through Yogic Mindfulness in Early Ayurveda," in *Yoga in Practice*, ed. David Gordon White (Princeton, NJ: Princeton University Press, 2011), 34–35.

4. Surendranath Dasgupta, *A History of Indian Philosophy*, vol. 1 (Cambridge: Cambridge University Press, 1922; Delhi: Motilal Banarsidass, 1975), 1975 edition, 230.

5. Gerald James Larson and Ram Shankar Bhattacharya, eds., *Yoga: India's Philosophy of Meditation* (Delhi: Motilal Banarsidass, 2008), 43.

6. Michel Angot, *Le Yoga-Sutra de Patanjali. Le Yoga-Bhasya de Vyasa avec des extraits du Yoga-Varttika de Vijnana-Bhiksu* (Paris: Les Belles Lettres, 2008), 24.

7. Ibid., 25–26.
8. Ibid., 60.
9. Lydia Polgreen, "Indian Who Built Yoga Empire Starts Work on Body Politic," *New York Times*, April 19, 2010.

SUGGESTIONS FOR FURTHER READING

CHAPTER I

An excellent critical overview of Indian philosophy is Richard King's *Indian Philosophy: An Introduction to Hindu and Buddhist Thought* (Edinburgh: Edinburgh University Press, 1999). Among the many books recently written on the *Yoga Sutra*, three that stand out are, first, the encyclopedic *Yoga: India's Philosophy of Meditation*, edited by Gerald James Larson and Ram Shankar Bhattacharya (Delhi: Motilal Banarsidass, 2008), which contains extensive translations and studies of nearly all of the major *Yoga Sutra* commentaries, from the fourth to the twentieth centuries. Second, Michel Angot's *Le Yoga-Sutra de Patanjali. Le Yoga-Bhasya de Vyasa avec des extraits du Yoga-Varttika de Vijnana-Bhiksu* (Paris: Les Belles Lettres, 2008) offers an exhaustive (and sometimes controversial) historical and theoretical treatment of the *Yoga Sutra*. And third, in his *The Yoga Sutras of Patanjali* (New York: North Point Press, 2009), Edwin Bryant translates and analyzes the *Yoga Sutra* in a "classical" commentarial format.

CHAPTER 2

In *An Introduction to the Yogasutra* (Delhi: Bharatiya Vidya Prakasana, 1985), Ram Shankar Bhattacharya situates the *Yoga Sutra* within the broader context of early Yoga traditions, and provides several valuable insights into the "historical Patanjali." Sensitive and insightful treatments of several of the philosophical issues raised in this chapter are found in Stuart Sarbacker, *Samadhi: The Numinous and Cessative in Indo-Tibetan Yoga* (Albany: State University of New York Press, 2005); and Gaspar M. Koelmans, *Patanjali's Yoga: From Related Ego to Absolute Self* (Pune: Papal Athenaeum, 1970).

CHAPTER 3

The full text of Colebrooke's studies of Hindu India's six philosophical schools may be found in Henry Thomas Colebrooke, *Miscellaneous Essays* (London: W. H. Allen, 1837), 1: 227–419. A scanned copy of volume one of this book, made available online from the library of Harvard University, may be accessed through GoogleBooks: http://books.google.com/books?vid=OCLC04738624&id=ay7l MFRLy20C&pg=PA1&lpg=PA1&dq=inauthor:Henry+inauthor:Thomas+inauthor:Colebrooke&as_brr=1#v=onepage&q&f=false. Background on the lives and Sanskrit training of the British Orientalists may be found in Rosane Rocher, "British Orientalism in the Eighteenth Century," and David Ludden, "Oriental Empiricism: Transformations in Colonial Knowledge," both in *Orientalism and the Post-Colonial Predicament: Perspectives on South Asia*, ed. Carol Breckenridge and Peter van der Veer (Philadelphia: University of Pennsylvania Press, 1993); and in David Kopf, *British Orientalism and the Bengal Renaissance: The Dynamics of Indian Modernization, 1773–1835* (Berkeley: University of California Press, 1969). Rocher's recent monograph *The Making of Western Indology: Henry Thomas Colebrooke and the East India Company* (New York: Routledge, 2012), coauthored with her husband Ludo Rocher, is a detailed and heavily annotated biography of Colebrooke. The history of Indian and European perceptions of yogis is documented in David Gordon White, *Sinister Yogis* (Chicago: University of Chicago Press, 2009), 198–254. A recent PhD dissertation on the nineteenth-century translators of the *Yoga Sutra* is Peter Michael Valdina, "Reading the *Yoga Sutra* in Colonial India" (Emory University, 2013).

CHAPTER 4

Herbert Herring provides an excellent historical and philosophical introduction to his bilingual (German and English) edition of our primary source for Hegel's interpretation of Yoga philosophy and the *Yoga Sutra*. This was Hegel's "review" of two lectures by Von Humboldt on the *Bhagavad Gita*: Georg Wilhelm Freidrich Hegel, *On the Episode of the Mahabharata Known by the Name Bhagavad-Gita by Wilhelm von Humboldt, Berlin 1826* (New Delhi: Indian Council of Philosophical Research, 1995). Two penetrating studies of Hegel's theories on Yoga philosophy and its place in the history of philosophy are Robert Bernasconi, "With What Must the History of Philosophy Begin? Hegel's Role in the Debate on the Place of India within the History of Philosophy," in *Hegel's History of Philosophy*, ed. David A.

Duquette (Albany: State University of New York Press, 2003), 35–49; and Michel Hulin, *Hegel et l'Orient suivi de la traduction annotée d'un essai de Hegel sur la Bhagavad-Gita* (Paris: J. Vrin, 1979). Two excellent critical surveys of the religious and philosophical encounters between India and the West are Ronald Inden, *Imagining India* (Oxford: Blackwell, 1990) and Wilhelm Halbfass, *India and Europe: An Essay in Understanding* (Albany: State University of New York Press, 1988). Chapters 5 through 9 of the latter work focus on the place of India in eighteenth- and nineteenth-century German philosophy.

CHAPTER 5

Rajendralal Mitra's masterful translation of the *Yoga Sutra* with the commentary of Raja Bhoja, prefaced by an exhaustive introduction to the text, its author, and Yoga philosophy, has been out of print for nearly a century, and is nearly impossible to find: *The Yoga Aphorisms of Patanjali* (Kolkata: Asiatic Society of Bengal, 1883).

CHAPTER 6

The story of the Theosophists' impact on Western and Indian appreciations of Yoga philosophy is best told by Catherine Albanese in chapter 6 ("Metaphysical Asia") of her *A Republic of Mind and Spirit: A Cultural History of American Metaphysical Religion* (New Haven, CT: Yale University Press, 2007), 330–93; and by Elizabeth De Michelis in *A History of Modern Yoga: Patañjali and Western Esotericism* (New York and London: Continuum, 2004). A blow-by-blow account of the scandals that beset Madame Blavatsky in Europe and India is contained in J. N. Farquhar, *Modern Religious Movements in India* (New York: Macmillan, 1915; Delhi: Munshiram Manoharlal, 1967), 1915 edition, 208–67. Blavatsky's collected writings are accessible online at http://www.katinkahesselink.net/blavatsky/. The most concise overview of the history of the terms *Hatha Yoga* and *Raja Yoga* may be found in two recent studies by Jason Birch: "The Meaning of Hatha in Early Hathayoga," *Journal of the American Oriental Society* 131, no. 4 (2011): 527–54; and "Rajayoga: The Reincarnations of the King of All Yogas," *International Journal of Hindu Studies* (forthcoming 2014).

CHAPTER 7

Swami Vivekananda's 1896 *Raja-Yoga: Conquering the Internal Nature* has gone into multiple editions. It may be found in volume one of his nine-volume *Complete Works*, online at http://www.advaitaashrama.org/cw/content.php. His other writings, correspondence, and lectures on Yoga are also found in these volumes. Elizabeth De Michelis's *A History of Modern Yoga: Patañjali and Western Esotericism* (New York and London: Continuum, 2004) is the most comprehensive guide to Vivekananda's life, influences, and teachings with respect to Yoga. An engaging account of Vivekananda's American years and his enduring legacy is contained in chapters 2 and 3 of Stefanie Syman's *The Subtle Body: The Story of Yoga in America* (New York: Farrar, Straus and Giroux, 2010). Vivekananda's idiosyncratic account of "evolution" in *Yoga Sutra* 4.2–3 is the subject of Dermot H.

Killingly's excellent study, "*Yoga-Sutra* IV, 2–3 and Vivekananda's Interpretation of Evolution," *Journal of Indian
Philosophy* 18 (1990): 151–79.

CHAPTER 8

On the Islamic pedigree of the Sahaj Marg's founding teachers, see especially Thomas Dahnhardt, *Change and Continuity in Indian Sufism: A Naqshbandi-Mujaddidi Branch in
the Hindu Environment* (New Delhi: D. K. Printworld,
2002). Abu'l Fazl's overview of the *Yoga Sutra* is translated
by Colonel H. S. Jarrett in *The Ain i Akbari by Abul Fazl-i-
Allami, Translated from the Original Persian* (Kolkata: Baptist Mission Press, 1894), 3: 183–98. The fascination with
yoga of the Mughal emperor Akbar's ill-fated great-
grandson Dara Shukuh is documented in Craig Davis, "The
Yogic Exercises of the 17th Century Sufis," in *Theory and
Practice of Yoga: Essays in Honour of Gerald James Larson*,
ed. Knut Jacobsen (Leiden: Brill, 2005), 303–16. Alberuni's
Arabic-language version of the *Yoga Sutra* has been translated with an exhaustive critical apparatus by Shlomo Pines
and Tuvia Gelblum in the *Bulletin of the School of Oriental
and African Studies* 29, no. 2 (1966): 302–25; 40, no. 3
(1977): 522–49; 46, no. 2 (1983): 258–304; and 52, no. 2
(1989): 265–305.

CHAPTER 9

The Yoga works of the Jain authors Haribhadra and Hemachandra have been translated in full with extensive intro-
ductions and commentary by Christopher Key Chapple
and John Thomas Casey in *Reconciling Yogas: Haribhadra's*

Collection of Views on Yoga. (Albany: State University of New York Press, 2003) and by Olle Qvarnström in *The Yogasastra of Hemacandra: A Twelfth-Century Handbook on Svetambara Jainism* (Cambridge, MA: distributed by Harvard University Press, 2002). Andrea Acri's pioneering study and translation of the Old Javanese-language *Dharma Patanjala* has recently been published under the title *Dharma Patanjala: A Saiva Scripture from Ancient Java Studied in the Light of Related Old Javanese and Sanskrit Texts* (Groningen: Egbert Forsten, 2013). The Shrivaishnava theologian Ramanuja's critiques of Yoga philosophy are treated in Robert Lester, *Ramanuja on the Yoga* (Chennai: Adyar Library and Research Centre, 1976).

CHAPTER 10

Friedrich Max Müller's 1899 classic *The Six Systems of Indian Philosophy* (New York: Longmans, Green,) can be accessed online at http://archive.org/details/sixsystemsofindi00mul liala.

CHAPTER 11

James Haughton Woods's *The Yoga-System of Patanjali* (Cambridge, MA: Harvard University Press, 1914), considered by scholars to be the finest translation of the *Yoga Sutra* (together with the commentaries of Vyasa and Vachaspati Mishra), is accessible online at http://archive.org/details /yogasystemofpata00woodu0ft. Joseph Alter's *Yoga in Modern India: The Body between Science and Philosophy* (Princeton, NJ: Princeton University Press, 2004) is a seminal study on the Yoga Renaissance and the medicalization of yoga in India mainly during the first half of the twentieth century. Mircea Eliade, whose Yoga "bedfellows" included the Nazi Jakob Wilhelm Hauer, the Indian philosopher Surendranath Dasgupta, and the yoga guru Sivananda, was the author of *Yoga, Immortality, and Freedom* (New York: Bollingen Foundation, 1958; Princeton, NJ: Princeton University Press, 2009), the most important twentieth-century synthesis of all of India's Yoga traditions. The poet T. S. Eliot's fascination with the Sanskrit language and the *Yoga Sutra* is documented in Cleo McNelly Kearns, *T. S. Eliot and Indic Traditions: A Study in Poetry and Belief* (Cambridge: Cambridge University Press, 1987). For the story of Jung's changing attitudes toward Yoga philosophy, see chapter 6 of Harold Coward's *Yoga and Psychology: Language, Memory, and Mysticism* (Albany: State University of New York Press, 2002).

CHAPTER 12

Four authorized biographies of T. M. Krishnamacharya have been authored by his son T.K.V. Desikachar and his grandson Kausthub Desikachar. The first, written by his son before Krishnamacharya's death in 1989, is titled *The Yoga of T. Krishnamacharya* (Chennai: Krishnamacharya Yoga Mandiram, 1982). This was followed in 1997 by *Sri Krishnamacharya the Purnacarya* (New York: Aperture, 1997); *Health, Healing, and Beyond: Yoga and the Living Tradition of Krishnamacharya*, with R. H. Cravens (New York: Aperture, 1998); and Kausthub Desikachar's *The Yoga of the Yogi: The Legacy of T. Krishnamacharya* (Chennai: Krishnamacharya Yoga Mandiram, 2005). Most recently, another authorized biography has been brought out by A. G. Mohan and

Ganesh Mohan: *Krishnamacharya: His Life and Teachings* (Boston: Shambhala, 2010). Mark Singleton has written a somewhat more critical approach to Krishnamacharya's life and legacy in chapter 9 of his *Yoga Body: The Origins of Modern Posture Practice* (New York: Oxford University Press, 2010). A groundbreaking work on Krishnamacharya's decades as yoga master at the Mysore Palace is Norman Sjoman's *The Yoga Tradition of the Mysore Palace* (New Delhi: Abhinav Publications, 1996). Further background on Krishnamacharya's life and his sometimes difficult relationship with his three most illustrious pupils may be found in Elizabeth Kadetsky's ethnohistorical memoir *First There Is a Mountain: A Yoga Romance* (Boston: Little, Brown, 2004). Three of Krishnamacharya's books have been translated into English. The 1934 *Yoga Makaranda* ("Emerald of Yoga") has been translated into English by T.K.V. Desikachar under the title *Yoga Makaranda: The Nectar of Yoga* (Chennai: Krishnamacharya Healing and Yoga Foundation, 2011), and by Nandini Ranganathan and Lakshmi Ranganathan as *Yoga Makaranda or Yoga Saram (The Essence of Yoga)*. The latter translation can be accessed online at http://grim mly2007.blogspot.com/2011/04/krishnamacharyas-yoga -makaranda-at-last.html. An abridged translation, by M. Narasimhan and M. A. Jayashree, with an introduction by Mark Singleton, is contained in David Gordon White, ed., *Yoga in Practice* (Princeton, NJ: Princeton University Press, 2011), 337–52. English language translations of Krishnamacharya's *Yoganjalisaram* ("Essential Benediction of Yoga") as well as his *Yoga Rahasya* ("Secret Teaching of Yoga") were posthumously published by the Krishnamacharya Yoga Mandiram in 1995 and 1998. The *Yoganjalisaram* is also contained in T.K.V. Desikachar, *The Heart of Yoga: Developing a*

Personal Practice (Rochester, VT: Inner Traditions International, 1999). The *Yoga Rahasya* ("Secret Teaching of Yoga"), which the entranced Krishnamacharya received directly from the tenth-century guru Nathamuni, was published in 1998 in Chennai by the Krishnamacharya Yoga Mandiram. Swami Hariharananda Aranya's excellent 1911 *Bhasvati* ("Dawning Sun") commentary on the *Yoga Sutra* was translated into English in 1963 as *Yoga Philosophy of Patanjali*, ed. Paresh Nath Mukherji (Kolkata: University of Kolkata). An American edition was brought out by the State University of New York Press in 1983.

CHAPTER 13

Georg Feuerstein's two groundbreaking studies of the *Yoga Sutra* and Yoga philosophy are *The Yoga Sutras: An Exercise in the Methodology of Textual Analysis* (New Delhi: Arnold Heinemann, 1979; Folkestone, Kent, England: Dowson and Sons, 1979) and *The Philosophy of Classical Yoga* (New York: St. Martin's Press, 1980). The most important recent theories concerning the identities of Patanjali and Vyasa are found in Philipp André Maas's introduction to his *Samadhipada: Das erste Kapitel des Patanjalayogasastra zum ersten Mal kritisch ediert* (Aachen: Shaker Verlag, 2006) and two articles by Johannes Bronkhorst: "Yoga and Sesvara Samkhya," *Journal of Indian Philosophy* 9 (1981): 309–20, and "Patanjali and the Yoga Sutras," *Studien zur Indologie und Iranistik* 10 (1985): 191–212. Strong arguments for the Buddhist origins of the *Yoga Sutra* and Yoga philosophy are Dominik Wujastyk, "The Path to Liberation through Yogic Mindfulness in Early Ayurveda," in *Yoga in Practice*, ed. David Gordon White (Princeton, NJ: Princeton University

Press, 2011), 31–42; and Michel Angot's introduction to his *Le Yoga-Sutra de Patanjali. Le Yoga-Bhasya de Vyasa avec des extraits du Yoga-Varttika de Vijnana-Bhiksu* (Paris: Les Belles Lettres, 2008).

Ayurveda, 36. See also
  Charaka Samhita

Dualism, 19, 27, 31, 47, 117, 170
Dutt, Romesh Chunder, 64

ego, 11, 28, 29, 30, 139, 190
eight-part practice, 5, 6, 13,
    33–34, 46, 47, 51, 93, 100,
    113, 114–15, 128, 131, 133,
    134, 150, 160–62, 164, 169,
    170, 176, 201, 202, 216, 219,
    226
Eliade, Mircea, 187–91, 194
Eliot, T. S., 193–94
"Emerald of Yoga." See *Yoga
    Makaranda* of Krishnam-
    acharya
entering other bodies, 31, 139–
    41, 195
entities. See *tattva*s
"Essential Benediction of
    Yoga." See *Yoganjalisaram*
    of Krishnamacharya
ether, 130
evolution. *See* Vivekananda,
    theory of evolution
"Expert Guide to the True
    Principles." See *Tattvavai-
    sharadi* of Vachaspati
    Mishra
"Explanation of Yoga." See
    Yogavarttika of Vijnana-
    bhikshu
"Exposition of the Commen-
    tary on the Yoga Teaching
    of Patanjali." See *Patanja-*

*layogashastrabhashyaviva-
rana* of Shankara

fakirs, 70, 71
fanatical, Yoga philosophy as,
    62–65, 68, 70, 71, 74
Feuerstein, Georg, 225–26
flight, 31, 138, 195–96
Fort William, 54, 59
Fox sisters, 103

Gheranda Samhita, 106
"Golden Embryo's Treatise on
    Yoga." See *Hiranyagarbha-
    yogashastra*
Gonika, 36, 38, 39, 68
"Great Commentary." See
    Mahabhashya of Patanjali
Greeks and Greek thought,
    58, 84, 60, 83, 84, 101, 129,
    175
Grinshpon, Yohanan, 225

Hall, Fitzedward, 63–64, 70
Haribhadra, 160, 161, 256
harmonial religion, 122, 129
Hastings, Warren, 54, 55, 56,
    57
Hatha Yoga, 4, 22, 46, 49, 64,
    76, 78, 79, 100, 106, 110,
    112–15, 127, 128, 130–33,
    144, 150, 151, 162, 186, 188,
    202
Hathayoga Pradipika of Svat-

maraman, 106, 107, 115, 127, 129, 186

Hauer, Jakob Wilhelm, 189–90

health, yoga and, 46, 130, 142, 185, 186, 197, 202, 210, 211

Heehs, Peter, 184

Hegel, Georg Wilhelm Friedrich, 81–91, 105, 121, 172, 189

Hemachandra, 9, 160, 161, 162

Himalayas, 17, 74, 99, 103, 109, 123, 185, 186, 187, 198, 207, 217. *See also* Kailash

Hindu law, 20, 51, 55, 56, 58, 59. See also *Krityakalpataru* of Lakshmidhara

Hiranyagarbha, 9, 13, 16, 21, 40, 43, 46, 51

Hiranyagarbhayogashastra, 21

Humboldt, Wilhelm von, 82–90

India Office Library, 75

Indonesia, 22, 44, 164–66. See also *Dharma Patanjala*; Java; Old Javanese

intellect, 11, 30, 31, 156

invisibility, 31

Isherwood, Christopher, 40, 192

Ishvara, 22, 33, 42, 45, 46, 48, 49, 51, 52, 61, 95, 118, 140, 155, 164, 165, 170, 172–81,

226, 228–29. *See also* Master of Yoga, Ishvara as; *pranidhana*; *seshvara samkhya*

Ishvara Krishna. See *Samkhya Karika* of Ishvara Krishna

Islam and Islamic culture, 51, 55, 59, 143–58, 164. *See also* Naqshbandis; Shi'a Islam; Sunni Islam; Sufi Islam

isolation, 28–30, 47, 48, 52, 89, 90, 98, 101, 164, 168, 178, 184, 225

Iyangar, Shrinivasa, 107, 129

Iyengar, B.K.S., 36, 38, 39, 40, 68, 195, 197, 201, 212, 216, 223

Jacobi, Hermann, 228

Jains and Jainism, 9, 19, 23, 25, 34, 141, 148, 160–62, 234. *See also* Haribhadra; Hemachandra

Java, 165, 166, 167, 232

Jha, Ganganath, 106, 173, 204, 205, 206, 207, 220

Jha, Muralidhara, 207

Jones, Sir William, 56–59

Judge, William Quan, 103, 105, 127, 172, 194

judicial review, 8, 27, 52, 137

Jung, Carl Gustav, 189, 190, 194

Kailash, 206, 208, 219, 220, 221

pandits, 56, 57, 61, 71, 73, 74, 75, 77, 92, 98–100, 117, 128, 142, 149, 150, 192, 200, 202, 203, 206

Panini, 10, 36

Pashupata Sutras, 169

Pashupatas and Pashupata Yoga, 22, 46, 134, 166, 167, 168, 169, 170, 171

Patancali, 37

Patanjala, Rishi, 73

Patanjalayogashastrabhashyavivarana of Shankara 41, 42, 45, 160

Patanjali Charita of Ramabhadra Dikshita, 38

Pattabhi Jois, K., 197, 201, 208, 216

Paul, N. C., 113–14

perfect concentration. See *samadhi*

Persian language and culture, 55, 147, 149, 150, 153

Person. *See* Purusha

Plato, 102

Pollack, Sheldon, 51

postural yoga, 9, 1, 185, 197

Prabhavananda, Swami, 40, 192

Prakriti, 11, 18, 27–32, 45, 47, 52, 95–98, 101, 135, 136, 164, 168, 178, 184; as dancer or actress, 28, 32; as *drshya*, "What is Seen," 28

prana, 107, 129, 130, 186

pranayama. See breath control

pranidhana, 33, 177–81, 215

principles. See *tattvas*

proto Modern Yoga, 120–21

psychoanalysis and psychology, 189–90, 193

Puranas, 5, 6, 20, 21, 22, 35, 44–48 51, 99, 100, 101, 114, 115, 117, 127, 128, 131, 133, 134, 140, 142, 155, 157, 158, 163, 165, 166, 167, 169, 171, 177, 178, 181, 233. See also *Kurma Purana; Linga Purana; Vishnudharmottara Purana*

pure contemplation. See *samadhi*

Purohit Swami, Shri, 192–93

Purusha, 11, 18, 27–32, 42, 43, 45, 47, 48, 52, 81, 84, 85, 95–98, 101, 118, 136, 164, 168, 178, 180, 184, 214. *See also* Spectator, Purusha as

Qualified Non-Dualism, 11, 19, 45, 111, 163, 201, 218, 219

Raja Yoga, 12, 106, 109–15, 124–34, 145, 151, 162, 172, 186, 187, 202

Raja Yoga (The) of Swami Vivekananda, 124–30, 133, 134, 187

Shankara or Shankaracharya, 19, 28, 32, 40–42, 45, 110, 111, 115, 141, 160, 177. See also *Aparoksanubhuti*; *Patanjalayogashastra-bhashyavivarana*
Shankarananda, Swami, 16
Sharngadhara Paddhati, 114
Shastri Deva, Govinda, 92, 105, 173
Shi'a Islam, 147, 149
Shimla, 205, 220, 221, 222
Shiva, 22, 37, 39, 46, 52, 106, 133, 134, 153, 155, 165–70
Shiva Samhita, 106, 127
"Shiva's Collection." See *Shiva Samhita*
"Short Statement on the Essence of Yoga." See *Yoga-sarasamgraha* of Vijnana-bhikshu
Shrivaishnavas, 160, 163, 198, 200, 218, 219
shruti, 20, 40, 211, 213
Siddhas, 114, 217
Singleton, Mark, 126, 142, 202
Sivananda, Swami, 186–88
six systems, 19, 59, 61, 63, 74, 76, 117. *See also* Mimamsa; Nyaya; Samkhya; Vaishe-shika; Vedanta
six-part practice, 46, 169
Sjoman, Norman, 220
Smritis. *See* Hindu law
soteriology. *See* liberation

Spectator, Purusha as, 28–30, 32
Spirit. *See* Purusha
spiritualism, 103, 106, 108, 109, 116, 118, 122, 123, 125, 129, 130, 142
Staff-Bearers. *See* Dandins
Starr, S. Frederick, 152
substrates. See *tattvas*
subtle body, 150. See also *chakras*; *kundalini*; *nadis*
Sufi Islam, 143, 144, 145, 147, 149, 151, 156
Sunni Islam, 147
supernatural powers, 11, 26, 31, 65, 68, 138, 139, 164, 170, 182, 185, 194, 195, 196, 217. *See also* direct yogic perception; entering other bodies; flight; invisibility; knowledge of past and future lives; mind reading
svadhyaya, 33, 215–16

Tagore, Debendranath, 116
Tamil language and culture, 37, 104, 111, 160, 163, 216
Tamil Nadu, 37, 104, 111, 163. *See also* Chennai; Cidam-baram
Tantra, 20, 64, 70, 99–101, 121, 142, 144, 169, 170, 171, 181
Tantric Yoga, 16, 22, 46, 49, 68, 76, 78, 79, 113, 114, 131,